There's an Addict in

D1430316

The Truth about Addiction from a Doctor in Recovery

By Herbert C. Munden, M.D.

Addict   Physician   Addictionologist

Copyright © 2012 by Herbert C. Munden, M.D

Updated and edited, June 2017, by Mary Ann Roser

Illustrations and paintings by Hannah G. Munden

All rights reserved. No part of this book may be reproduced or transmitted in any form or by any means without written permission from the author or his estate.

ISBN (978-0-9882371-62)

ISBN(0988237164)

Printed in USA

Dedication

This is dedicated to all those who work in addiction treatment and who I urge to never give up on anyone; to my wife, Hannah, who hung in there with me when it would have been so much easier to move on; and to my three children, Marshall, Shannon, and Vanessa, for giving me something to live for when times were dark.

Also to Travis Morford, Marshall Gwin, and their families. Travis and Marshall died from this disease. Marshall was the brother I never had.

I thank God for the opportunity to share what I've learned. It has been quite a ride, but even if I could, I would not change a thing. I could have missed the pain, but then I would have missed the dance.

Table of Contents

Foreword   7

Preface   8

Introduction   11

Chapter 1: Changing Old Beliefs   14

Chapter 2: Chemical Dependency Is a Disease   18

Chapter 3: Many Factors Contribute to the Disease   26

Chapter 4: How to Decide if a Loved One Has This Disease   34

Chapter 5: Physical Consequences of Chemical Use   52

Chapter 6: How to Identify the Chemically Dependent Person   63

Chapter 7: The Family   70

Chapter 8: For Parents of Chemically Dependent Children   83

Chapter 9: Matching the Patient to Treatment   93

Chapter 10: The Power of the Environment   102

Chapter 11: Sobriety   108

Chapter 12: Simple Directions   115

Chapter 13: Random Drug Screening   124

Chapter 14: Adult Children of Alcoholics   129

Chapter 15: Barriers to Success   132

Chapter 16: To the Doctors   138

Chapter 17: The Criminal Justice System and the Disease   *146*

Chapter 18: The Suboxone Breakthrough   *151*

Chapter 19: How to Find a Treatment Center   *156*

Chapter 20: Closing Thoughts   *163*

Afterword   *166*

Acknowledgements   *168*

Glossary   *169*

Opioid Facts   *171*

Post-Operative Pain Management   *175*

Foreword

When my husband, Herbert C. "Butch" Munden, started working on this book in 2012, I had no idea what he was doing. He would come home from work and spend the entire evening holed up in a little house in our backyard. He built the "little house" years ago and even lived in it. That was before I got serious about Al-Anon, and we began to get along better.

After several weeks, he informed the family of his little secret: He was writing a book. He said it was on addiction but did not elaborate. When he completed the manuscript, he asked me to read it. Of course, I was curious about what he had been writing in that little house, but I have to say I was not too excited to read a book about addiction. I worked in the office with him, and we certainly have had a significant number of alcoholics and addicts in our own family!

I was stunned as I began to read his manuscript. I did not want to put it down. He captured me with his stories and his own experiences. At this point, we had been married for thirty-four years, but there was still a lot I didn't know. His presentation of the medical information was not too technical for me to understand. I could see how anyone reading this book would find it useful. Who has not had an addict in the closet and needs to know the truth about this disease?

Preface

On May 19, 1985, I walked into a treatment center in Atlanta, Georgia. The first person I met looked at me and said: "You are here because you are sick. You are not a bad person." I had no idea what he was talking about. Nor was I all that interested in finding out. I really didn't care whether I lived or died because shame, depression, and fear were controlling my life. Thus began a journey down paths unknown and terrifying.

Many people had commented that because I was a medical doctor, I should have known that I was the "textbook" picture of an alcoholic and a drug addict. I did not know that, and even if I had any idea, it probably would not have prevented the course I was on. I believed that an alcoholic was a person who stayed drunk most of the time and that he or she was not capable of holding a job or taking care of the family. I was sure that drug addicts were people who shot heroin and could not function in life. They broke into your house and robbed liquor stores.

The education I received in medical school on this topic amounted to a one-hour lecture. Sadly, the vast majority of today's medical schools do not provide much, if any, training about alcohol and drug addiction. The students spend weeks, if not months, learning about diabetes, heart disease, and all of the other medical maladies that afflict humanity. Most people assume that the majority of physicians should be able to identify and recommend treatment for someone who is addicted to alcohol or drugs. Sadly, that is not the case. I have no good answer on why the medical profession remains ignorant about a disease that affects 10 percent to 12 percent of our society. Due to the prevalence of addiction and the soaring number of overdose deaths we are seeing in cities and towns across America, efforts are now being made by groups across the country to hold drug manufacturers and medical institutions accountable. They are demanding training that is equal to the training that already exists for other chronic diseases. After all, drug overdose deaths for 2016 are expected to exceed 59,000 — a record increase and the sad legacy of an opioid epidemic sweeping our nation.

When I began thinking about writing this book, my intention was to produce an introductory textbook for medical professionals because, to my knowledge, such a book did not exist. My intention has since expanded to include those who are affected by this disease — addicts and their loved ones. My hope and prayer is that this book will help them find hope and understanding in these pages. I want them to know that this disease is treatable.

I mentioned that I have this disease. I do not intend to go into all the details and "war stories" of my eighteen years of addiction. Many others have written in great detail about the insanity and chaos of alcohol and drug addiction. But I do want to provide some context about how I went from being an addict to wanting to help others.

I started working in addiction medicine in 1986. I had not planned to pursue this path, but through a series of "coincidences," I found myself in charge of a chemical dependency treatment program in Austin, Texas. The psychiatrist who had helped start the program was frustrated and once told me that he couldn't understand why "all of these people lie to me, and they try to hide drugs everywhere." I had no problem understanding this behavior. I had done some of the same things. And so the journey began.

I brought with me a few important lessons. In medical school, I had learned something that I believed was a huge part of the "art" of medicine. A brilliant professor of mine had once said, "You must listen to the patient, truly listen, and they will tell you the diagnosis."

I was determined to do that. Looking back on my career, I can say that I listened hard, and I became educated. This book is not just about me. It is about what I have learned from listening to literally thousands of patients and their family members. They have taught me so much from their mistakes, struggles, and successes. I once told a friend that practicing addiction medicine was probably like practicing oncology. Incredible miracles sometimes happen, but, unfortunately, there are many tragic deaths. I do not claim in any way to be the "authority" on addiction medicine. I am sure many could argue or disagree with what I say in this book. But I am relying on facts and experience here. The old phrase "Don't shoot the messenger" is about the only defense I can summon! I am currently battling cancer and it is likely that I won't be around if, by some miracle, this book ever goes to print. So I really don't give a damn what disagreements there may be.

Introduction

My dream for the past fourteen years has been to have an opportunity to teach medical students about chemical dependency. The opportunity has not been available, and I do not see it happening in my lifetime. On August 12, 2011, I was diagnosed with metastatic prostate cancer. I have had to step back from many activities and focus on what I must do. I have looked at my faith and at what is important in my life. I have had to set priorities. I have no idea how much time I have left, but celebrating my hundredth birthday is not likely. Hold the candles.

Six months ago, one of my patients who works in the recording industry offered me an opportunity to record what I have seen and learned in my work. We had briefly talked about my cancer, and he encouraged me to share my knowledge so that others could benefit from my experience. I could not make a connection at that point, but several months later, it came to me. I could teach, but not in the way I had planned. How I could do that became clear that evening in a matter of moments. I spent years not listening to my heart but even I could hear this message! The answer was this book.

I know the disease of chemical dependency because I have it. I am certain chemical dependency is a treatable illness because thousands of people, including myself, have been treated successfully. Awareness must come followed by willingness, and then the student becomes teachable.

I will do my best to teach you how to spot this disease. It's clear if you have some understanding of what you are looking for. You won't detect a rash or a cough, or any other visible evidence, but the symptoms are glaring. I will show you how you can help yourself and your loved one. You will no longer feel helpless. I want people to learn that talking about this disease is OK and that shame and embarrassment are a waste of time and energy. I want people to know the real truth about this disease, however difficult this may be. I want people to understand that

11

medical professionals are poorly trained about addiction and can't be trusted to provide appropriate treatments when they have so little knowledge. Most of all, I want those who have this disease to know there is hope. I cannot teach hope, but I can direct a person down a path that leads to hope.

If you read this book because you need help, I believe it will lessen your pain and fear. You will be able to pass the knowledge on to others who are suffering because of this disease. To echo the famous biblical quote, "Then you will know the truth, and the truth will set you free." You have the right to be free and happy. Whether you are a family member, friend, or the person who has this disease, joy is within your reach. No one has to be doomed to a lifelong prison of addiction.

Alcoholism has nothing to do with willpower, intellect, or morality

Chapter 1: Changing Old Beliefs

Most of us have been taught, directly or indirectly, that alcoholics and addicts have something "wrong" with them. This "wrong" may be a lack of intelligence or willpower; others believe it's a moral failing. They might cluck their tongues and say, "This would not have happened if she had only gone to church more or if he had not been influenced by undesirables." The blame and rationalizations persist, even among medical professionals. The good news is that things are improving slightly. The American Society of Addiction Medicine and similar organizations are working diligently to change an ingrained perception that has been around for hundreds, if not thousands, of years.

Psychiatric illness has always been categorized with alcohol and drug addiction. In the 1950s that began to change, and, today, most people readily accept psychiatric illness as being a disease. This change resulted when Thorazine, the first antipsychotic medication, was introduced. It was followed by other drugs, causing long-held beliefs about psychiatric illness to slowly dissolve. Our society became more accepting of mental illness simply because people saw that it could be treated. That meant something must be physically wrong in the brain, and it was not a choice. The shame and guilt began to lessen in patients and their family members. The patient was no longer hidden, literally, in some cases. And the guilt family members felt for thinking they had somehow contributed to their loved one's "insanity" began to fade.

But society's views on alcoholics and addicts didn't really change. The 1960s only added fuel to the fire. In just one generation, the idea of "better living through better chemistry" became entrenched in our society as an easy fix for whatever ails you. Pharmaceutical companies were producing hundreds of new medications with the promise of increasing lifespan and improving one's quality of life. Our medical schools were teaching young physicians that there was a pill, powder, or liquid that could fix any problem a patient might have. Times were changing and events were occurring that would create, what seemed to be, an explosion of alcoholics and drug addicts.

Fortunately, not everyone bought this view. I have often said that most meetings or conferences are a waste of time because the truly important information could have been presented in three minutes rather than two hours. There are memorable exceptions, one of which happened to me in 1973 during my second week of medical school. All of the naïve first-year medical students gathered in the auditorium for a presentation. To this day, I cannot recall the professor's name but I vividly remember what he said. He led into his lecture by saying, "If you make it through this institution," a phrase that scared the hell out of everyone. He then went on to say that, as physicians, we would meet thousands upon thousands of people who were sick. He then said that most of us would try to prescribe a medication because we were being trained in Western medicine. He noted that we would have a vast array of medications to treat whatever the complaint might be. We were told that there was nothing wrong with these medications for they had saved thousands of lives.

He said that patients' discomfort or "dis-ease" occurs because they are out of balance in some part of their lives. He went on to explain that there are three parts to human beings, which we must remember with every patient we see: the physical, the emotional, and the spiritual. Our greatest challenge as physicians was to do our best to help our patients regain a balance in their lives. We must take the time and have the courage to ask each patient how he or she is doing spiritually and emotionally. The physical part would be clear in most cases through examination and laboratory testing. Treating all aspects of the patient is the "art" of practicing medicine, he concluded. I have never forgotten his words and pray I never will.

15

It is so important for one to remember that chemical dependency is a multifactorial disease, meaning that multiple factors contribute to it. In that sense, it's like diabetes. I believe most people would not argue whether diabetes is a disease. We know that genetics plays a role in diabetes, and the severity of the disease varies greatly, from the rapidly progressive juvenile onset to the type 2 form, which is fairly easy to treat. We know that other factors, including diet, exercise, stress, and body weight are extremely important to the long-term prognosis. So it is with this disease of chemical dependency. All of the contributing factors must be addressed.

We have to move away from thinking the drug is the problem.

Chapter 2: Chemical Dependency Is a Disease

I have spent years describing the anatomy of the brain and the biochemical malfunctions present in addiction. I believe, for the most part, I have wasted much time. I do not think I have ever convinced any patient or family member that chemical dependency is a real disease. Family members nod their heads politely and quickly slip back into their old defense mechanisms, usually, denial and rationalization. Patients often think I have just given them an excuse for their behavior — until we come to the part about them taking responsibility for their disease. The ingrained belief that this problem is about intellect, willpower, or morality often persists to the point that the family will either disintegrate or the patient will end up in jail or dead.

Many books have been written for those who need proof that addiction is a disease. Two great examples are Dr. Carl Erickson's The Science of Addiction and the American Society of Addiction Medicine's The Principles of Addiction Medicine. I have seen hundreds of patients cling to their old beliefs that they could overcome their addiction to alcohol or drugs with their "plan," which they likely have tried before and is doomed to fail again. Many have died or disappeared. Those who survive may seek help months or years later, having run the gamut of arrests, divorces, job losses, and failing physical health. They remind me of the patients who see their doctor for diabetes and receive all of the current information and the best medications available only to say that they have a different plan they will follow to beat the disease. Some will argue that there are people who, with great effort, determination, and prayer, have conquered a seemingly terminal disease. I have had many patients who have asked me about that, and my response is, "Yes, I am sure this is true, but are you willing to take that risk?"

By the time they have come to me for help, there is no place for judgment. I simply ask, "How did your plan work?"

Understanding that you have a disease, whether it is diabetes or addiction, is very different than accepting it. Intellectually understanding the disease is not rocket science. The progression to acceptance, if it occurs, develops over time and requires a willingness to surrender old beliefs and open up the mind to new ones.

In 1969, Elisabeth Kübler-Ross wrote On Death and Dying, a seminal book on grief and loss. Kübler-Ross was the first physician to study the grieving process in-depth and report her findings. She defined grief as the real or perceived loss of something that is important in someone's life. Of course, she was studying the ultimate loss. In her interviews with terminally ill patients from various backgrounds, she found a remarkable similarity in how they approached death. Each experienced the same emotional stages: denial, bargaining, anger, depression, and acceptance. When individuals are told they have a serious disease or must give up something terribly important to them, the grieving process begins.

Most patients who come to my office are in the denial or bargaining stages. Both are difficult to deal with. It is important to understand that denial does not mean the person is lying. Denial is a psychological mechanism that we all use to protect ourselves from the pain of reality. We may experience denial after being told about the death of a loved one, a dear friend, or even a pet. Denial is so protective that the grieving person may even telephone the loved one, only to realize he or she is truly gone. Denial is extremely common in chemical dependency. Even to this day, I sit in awe of its power.

Similarly, bargaining is very difficult to deal with because patients think of new barriers to avoid giving up the thing they want. When it's the loss of a loved one, they'll say, "This would not have happened if only I had done X." If the thing they want is a drug, they might say, "I will quit X, but only if Y happens first."

One other psychological mechanism I'll mention briefly is rationalization. I derive a certain amount of amusement from listening to a patient's description of why he or she drank or drugged. I told a friend not too long ago that just when I think I have heard it all, someone wins the award. Comedian Bill Engvall used to do a comedy skit called, "Here's Your Sign." The sign read "I'm Stupid" and was awarded to the person who seemed to have the poorest judgment. The difference between the skit and addicts is the patients really believe they have a very plausible reason for their behavior. Only when they move beyond this and the other defense mechanisms will they be able to find healing.

Again, there is no place for judgment. But to help patients gain perspective, I have often commented, "Normal people do not do that."

Pleasure Reward Pathway

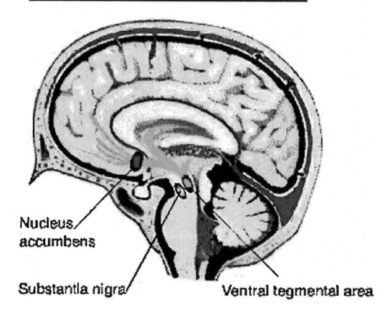

This depicts the part of the brain affected by chemical dependency.

I also want to stress two concepts that are very important for the family and the addicted person to understand. First, I mentioned that the proper term for this disease is chemical dependency. It is likely the terms "addict" and "alcoholic" will disappear from the literature. Chemical dependency exerts a powerful influence on the brain and changes it, just like cardiovascular disease changes the heart. We now know that the addiction pathology occurs in the mesolimbic center, the brain's pleasure and reward pathway. Often called the primitive or survival brain, repeated exposure to a substance or behavior leads to a surge of dopamine, a chemical messenger that plays a big role in motivating survival behavior (eating) as well as pleasure-seeking. With addiction, malfunctions occur in various parts of the mesolimbic center, including the nucleus accumbens, medial forebrain bundle, and the amygdala.

A great deal of argument has erupted over the years on how to define a mood-altering drug. In The Science of Addiction, Erickson says it is any chemical that causes the release of dopamine from the nucleus accumbens. As we learn more, this definition may expand, but for now it is amazingly accurate. In addiction medicine today, we consider alcohol as no different from Valium, heroin, or cocaine. That often shocks people.

When I entered treatment in 1985, I was clear with everyone that while I agreed I had a problem with opioids and cocaine, I was in no way addicted to alcohol and marijuana. I was totally ignorant about this disease. To my surprise and irritation, the treatment team advised me I had to abstain from alcohol and all other drugs. I was hoping there were other institutions that had a different opinion about this but I was never able to find one. A young man who once came to me for treatment was taking 240 milligrams of OxyContin per day and had been smoking marijuana every day for the past twelve years. When I told him the pot was also an equal contributor to his problem, he responded much as I did. With a dropped jaw, hands clenched, face pale, and sweat on his forehead, he managed to utter, "What the hell do you mean?" After a long discussion, he agreed to keep his mind open to this idea.

21

Cross-addiction is the term that has been used for years to describe this phenomenon. As ongoing research has provided significant information about this disease, I have been able to simplify my explanation of cross-addiction. Today I explain to patients it is not any one drug that is the problem. The trouble is a biochemical malfunction in the nucleus accumbens of the brain, and this part of the brain does not really give a damn whether it is alcohol, heroin, Valium, or cocaine. Anything will do.

But opioid or cocaine addicts typically believe they will be able to drink alcohol socially because "it" had never been a problem. They may use alcohol "socially" on many occasions, but, invariably, the time comes when their brain tells them they can do the same with opioids or cocaine without becoming addicted. This alcohol experiment may last weeks or months. They may even be able to use their old drug a time or two, but within days or weeks, they are back in the same position, a prisoner to their drug. It is described best by two words that appear in the Alcoholics Anonymous book, "cunning" and "baffling."

It is amazing to watch this process and the psychological thinking that goes with it. Sadly, many die from their disease because their pride often prevents them from making another attempt to get sober. Along with this is often an attitude of "I know what to do now," and this worsens the prognosis. Try as they may, addicts will find that their intellect alone is insufficient to cure the disease or keep it in remission.

My second point is, it is important to understand that there is a very wide variation in how the disease manifests itself. I mentioned earlier that most of us grew up with the notion that alcoholics and addicts are dangerous, unpredictable, live under bridges, etc. It is true; approximately 3 percent to 5 percent do fit this old definition. The vast majority does not. Perhaps the best way to explain this is by using the bell curve. Other diseases, besides addiction, such as diabetes and heart disease also would fit nicely into this model. The bell curve, simply put, means that some people (3 percent to 5 percent) have a severe form of the disease, another 3 percent to 5 percent have a very mild form, and everyone else is somewhere in between, or under the big, curved bell.

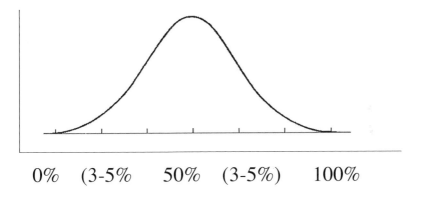

0%   (3-5%   50%   (3-5%)   100%

The ends of the bell show the outliers; the vast majority is in between.

As an example, you may know someone who has type 1, or juvenile-onset, diabetes. The prognosis is very poor for these people despite the advances in medicine. You may also know adults who develop diabetes later in life can do well by eating a healthier diet and losing weight. These two groups fall within the 3 percent to 5 percent darkened areas of the diagram. The larger group of people varies a great deal. Many factors determine whether a patient moves one way or the other, mild to severe or severe to mild. Because diabetes and addiction are chronic progressive diseases, they will get worse over time if there is no treatment.

This explanation can be a source of helpful rationalization for alcoholics and addicts. Many will tend to believe that they are "not as bad as" someone else. For many years, some members of Alcoholics Anonymous looked down their noses at drug addicts. Some AA members even asked them to leave the meetings. This attitude is seldom seen today. Someone once said that the AA members were

23

prejudiced, and if you believe that prejudice is simply ignorance, then they were correct. Chemical dependency is a predictable, chronic, progressive disease. You have it or you do not. If you do, it doesn't matter where you come in on the scale.

The certainty is that if you do not do something about it, then all of the negative consequences that have not yet happened eventually will. You can only be "a little bit" alcoholic or addict for a while. In the early stages of the disease, almost every alcoholic or addict will tell you that they were able to use alcohol or drugs socially, sometimes for years. At some point, though, things deteriorate, and that is truly baffling to the individual. I once had a patient who was a well-respected attorney who advised me that he had been a heavy drinker for thirty years. He outlined his various accomplishments over this period and, evidently, saw no reason to quit. After listening to his story, I pointed out that while his accomplishments were admirable, he had accumulated four DWIs in the past two years and there was a good chance he would be going to prison. He was still drinking alcohol at the time of this interview! Most of you have heard the old medical joke, "You can't be just a little bit pregnant." You also can't be a little bit alcoholic or drug-addicted.

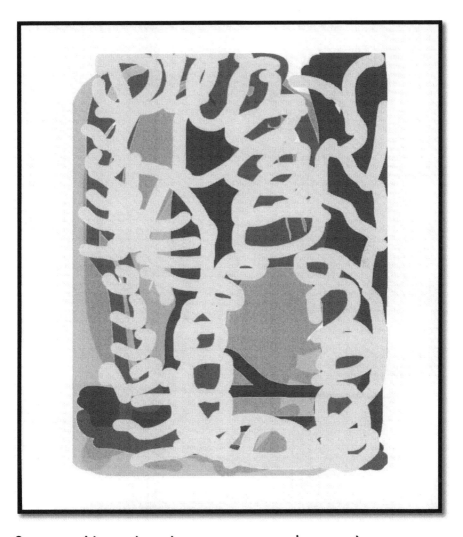

Some would say that physicians are our biggest drug dealers, and, collectively speaking, that may be true.

Chapter 3: Many Factors Contribute to the Disease

Earlier I mentioned that many factors contribute to the probability a person may develop chemical dependency. Here are the factors that I consider to be the most important:

(1) Genetics. We have known for years in medicine that inheritance plays some role in alcoholism. These statistics are important but complicated. Volumes have been written on this subject, so I will try to boil it down to the essentials.

We know today that multiple genes are involved in this disease. That helps us understand why there is such a wide variation in chemically dependent patients. Knowing this information also potentially allows us to develop medications that are gene-specific. About 10 percent to 12 percent of us who have this disease were born with the susceptibility. In other words, we were "wired" to develop it.

When giving lectures on chemical dependency, I would tell people that if they had children, it was very likely they would see this disease again. I would go on to tell them that the most important thing they could do for their children would be to stay sober so their children would know there is another option. This is so important because many children never hear of a family member who got sober. In my family, my father was an alcoholic, my mother was addicted to prescription medication, and all four of my grandparents were alcoholics. As far as I know, my sister was the only one in our family who did not have this disease. After watching my family, I did not know that sobriety was possible or that it was even an option.

(2) Society. Our society promotes, encourages, and glamorizes the use of chemicals. I do not believe that would surprise anyone. Drug and alcohol use by movie stars and musicians influences young people. They idolize celebrities. Add to this the pressure that these young people feel to "succeed" and become rich. Then add to that the increasing fear for personal safety in the face of news about

terrorist attacks and random mass shootings. You can understand why people are drawn to something that will alleviate their discomfort.

It is equally important to remember that peer pressure is alive and well. Some parents believe that if they move their child to a private school, this problem will be eliminated. Eventually, they come to realize the pressure and availability of drugs and alcohol are no different. Young people are using mood-altering drugs much earlier than we ever expected. We know with certainty that people who start using alcohol and drugs before or during their teenage years have a higher probability of developing this disease. Scientists have speculated that even those who were not predisposed to chemical dependency at birth had a higher probability of becoming dependent because the exposure to addictive substances damaged their genetic material. Others have argued the problem was due to early exposure to drugs, which caused alterations in the neuronal receptors, or nerve endings, that respond when stimulated. Either way, we are seeing a generation of young people who will suffer the consequences of this devastating disease.

The likelihood is high that a chemically dependent person will interact with the criminal justice system. We usually think of this with DWIs or drug possession charges. But we must also consider that people with chemical dependency may be arrested for burglary, assault, robbery, and so on. It is an expensive habit.

Unfortunately, most of the officials who run our criminal justice system have no understanding of this disease. But that's not surprising. If our medical professionals have no training in addiction, then why would we expect our law enforcement officers, lawyers, and judges to know more about it? Thankfully, a few professionals do understand that punishment alone is not likely to help the alcoholic or addict pursue sobriety. Some judges will encourage treatment as a means of keeping the person out of the revolving door of the criminal justice system. And some attorneys recognize that addiction is the common denominator in most of their clients' criminal charges. These lawyers will plead with the court system to consider treatment as part of the judge's final order.

Most of us know recidivism rates are high for those who have been to prison. There are many reasons, including a belief among some criminals that lawbreaking is their job. Consider the young man who has been arrested three, four, or even five times for theft, burglary, or DWI, all of which were brought on by his drug addiction. Understand that I am not making excuses for this person. Let us assume that this young man, if he were clean and sober, would not commit these crimes. His history before alcohol and drug use did not show any evidence of psychopathology. Afterward, he's a different person. The compulsion to use is so powerful that addicted individuals will lie, steal, cheat, and rob — as long as it's necessary to maintain their supply of the drug. With no treatment available, this young man is more than likely going to return to alcohol and drugs. He finds that his felony record prevents him from finding an apartment or a job. He returns to his old friends. What happens next is predictable: the revolving door.

Even with treatment the path forward won't be easy. He still will face the inability to get an apartment or a job, but he now has plans for the future and a degree of hope that moves him away from the revolving door. He has some positive influences in his life. He begins to want to change and is willing to work at it.

My hope is that our criminal justice system will consider that there is a solution to this disease and that those individuals who are truly pursuing sobriety should not have to live with always being classified as felons or criminals. Thank goodness for the thousands of men and women who are sober and who will tell you that being labeled a "convicted felon" is no excuse to drink or drug.

(3) The medical profession. Some would say that physicians are our biggest drug dealers, and, collectively speaking, that may be true. But the vast majority of physicians are very good at what they do. They are caring and compassionate and

would never knowingly harm a patient. "Knowingly" is the problem. I have already gone into detail about the lack of addiction education in our medical schools. The profession must someday take responsibility for this. That aside, we are seeing a tendency for physicians to prescribe increasingly more drugs, especially opioids and benzodiazepines. Perhaps there are legitimate reasons for this, but it is likely that time and convenience are part of the problem. It is much easier to write a prescription than it is to sit and talk with the patient. It is so common today for a patient complaining of pain to receive a prescription for a rather large number of pain pills, with refills. Many doctors have said that doing this prevents them from getting numerous calls from the patient for additional pain medication.

We know that some patients are simply doctor shopping, meaning they will see several doctors and obtain the same medication(s) from all of them. This behavior is discussed in the section describing opioid use disorder in the DSM-5, the Diagnostic and Statistical Manual of Mental Disorders on which doctors rely. Doctor shopping is not normal! Until recently physicians had no way of knowing that patients were seeing two, three, or more doctors. They only would find out if a pharmacist called or if they accidentally discovered this from family members. Computer technology is changing this, and as of mid-2017, every state but Missouri had a Physician Drug Monitoring Program, enabling doctors to check a database to see where else a patient might be getting prescription drugs. But not all states require doctors to check the database before prescribing, leaving a valuable tool unused.

Another problem is consumers can buy large amounts of drugs over the Internet. I once had a patient who said he didn't need to contact dealers; he had a computer that was more reliable. Our laws are slowly changing, but access to opioids, benzodiazepines, and stimulants is still just a click away for many alcoholics and addicts. We live in a society that provides the chemicals. Combine this with a genetic makeup that predisposes someone to have the disease of chemical dependency, and now the path is set for disaster.

Several years ago, a twenty-three-year-old man came to see me, struggling with alcoholism. His family was from Iraq, and the patient was born in the United States. His family had visited me first to tell me that they were worried about their son. They were very ashamed of him and were open in expressing how embarrassed they were about "his problem." The parents were very clear that there had never been such a problem in their families and that neither of them had even touched alcohol. They could not understand the "weakness" in their son. This is a perfect example of how society and perhaps religious or cultural beliefs can play a significant role in labeling the disease something it is not. It was likely true that there was no family history of the disease because they had lived in a culture and followed a religion that absolutely forbade using alcohol. When the parents said they did not have problems with alcohol, I asked the mother a simple question: "Since you have never used or abused alcohol, we really don't know whether you are an alcoholic or not, do we?" I don't know whether she could comprehend the question at that moment. The parents attended Al-Anon, and I feel sure that if we were to ask mom the same question today, she would have a different answer. Their son has been clean and sober for more than five years, and the family is proud of him and supportive.

(4) Psychological makeup. This is a very important factor in the disease, although it is highly controversial. As human beings, we are all different in many respects. I say this to every patient I meet because no two humans are exactly the same. We have different experiences, different backgrounds, and psychologically speaking, we don't have a duplicate copy of ourselves wandering around somewhere. Thank goodness.

It has been said that who we are is the result of the programming that has occurred in our lives. In other words, what we think and what we believe are, for the most part, a result of our life experiences. Anthony de Mello, the famous spiritual teacher and psychotherapist, once said we should think of the brain as being a computer that is empty at birth. Then the programming begins! It is usually our parents or family members who begin entering information into this computer. As we grow older, we have playmates and then we go to school. At school, we gather information from our teachers and different peer groups as well as from television and our computers. We have to deal with the turmoil of adolescence, young adulthood, and the workaday world. The pressures continue to mount. Then someday, some of us have the opportunity to stop and take an honest look at how we think and what we believe. We discover that some of our thoughts and beliefs are very bad or based on inaccurate information. The child who was told he was stupid and will never amount to anything continues to believe that because his inner computer keeps playing this part over and over. Escaping that damaging self-esteem loop requires great effort, but it can be done.

I will talk later about the 12-step program. For now, I want to focus solely on the fourth step. It states, "We make a searching and fearless moral inventory of ourselves." Perhaps moral is not the best word, but it is about the need to take an inventory of who we are, what we think, and what we believe.

We know today that the human brain has the capacity for neuroplasticity, or the ability to form and reorganize new pathways to compensate for injuries or incorrect thinking patterns. In recent years, some psychotherapists have begun using a fascinating treatment called eye movement desensitization and reprocessing, or EMDR, which uses rapid eye movements to create new circuits to change thinking patterns or long-standing beliefs. EMDR has been used on patients who have experienced trauma to dampen the emotional power of devastating memories. The old saying that you can't erase the tapes but you can tape over them is really not that far off. For years I have had patients tell me repeatedly, "This is just who I am." That may be so at that point, but we must come to understand that we are far more capable of changing than we have ever dreamed. The testaments to this are the thousands of individuals in recovery who have gone from hopelessness and negativity to a life that is full of meaning and hope. Quite simply, we are not stuck with who we are if we are willing to put forth some effort to change.

(5) The influence of other factors. Socioeconomic position may contribute to addiction in that we may see inhalant and alcohol use more often among lower-income groups and a tendency for cocaine use at higher-income levels. But socioeconomic status does not really contribute to determining disease probability. It really doesn't matter whether one is drinking expensive scotch or cheap wine. It is the alcohol that counts for the alcoholic, and the physical damage is the same.

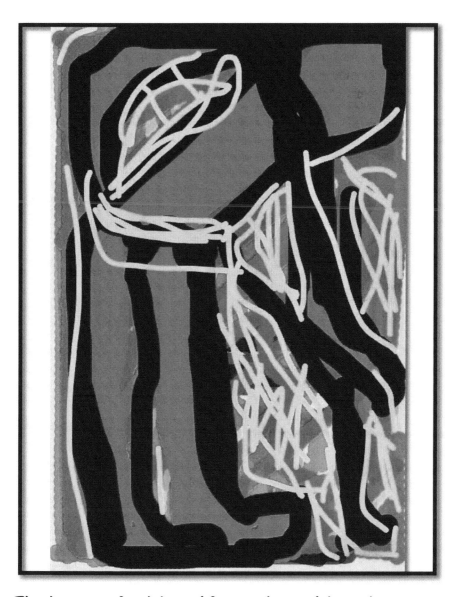

The duration of withdrawal from a chemical depends on its fat solubility, or the chemical's ability to be dissolved in fats or oil.

Chapter 4: How to Decide if a Loved One Has This Disease

When medical professionals diagnose someone with a disease, they may consult the most recent edition of the Diagnostic and Statistical Manual of Mental Disorders (DSM), which describes a given mental illness and provides a list of criteria that will confirm the diagnosis. This manual gives uniformity in developing an accurate diagnosis and provides the diagnostician with generally clear parameters. A disease, to be so classified, must fulfill one of the basic rules of medicine: "A disease has a group of signs or symptoms that are consistent from patient to patient." For example, in medical school, we learned that a patient who presents with the symptoms of night sweats, weight loss, and coughing up blood most likely has the diagnosis of tuberculosis. Further tests can prove or disprove the diagnosis. For a diabetic, the symptoms are excessive thirst, excessive hunger, and frequent trips to the bathroom at night to pass urine.

Chemical dependency is classified as a mental illness because the majority of symptoms are behavioral. The DSM is a wonderful book; however, there is a great deal of subjectivity with many of the criteria. In other words, physicians have to make decisions based on their opinion whether these symptoms are present. Complicating matters further is the fact that many mental illnesses have overlapping symptoms.

Chemical dependency is no exception. It often is misdiagnosed as a psychiatric illness and, by the same token, a psychiatric diagnosis may be misdiagnosed as chemical dependency. I recall asking a physician about this dilemma while I was in treatment. I was convinced I had psychiatric issues because several psychiatrists had told me so. He first asked me a very simple question: "Were you honest with the doctors about your alcohol and drug use?" No, I admitted. Then he said, "Well, you really don't know then. So why don't you stop using alcohol and drugs and then you will find out the" truth." Once I abstained from taking substances all of the psychiatric symptoms disappeared quickly. This is a generalization, I realize, but all I can say is that alcoholics and addicts tend to lie a great deal. We lie to cover the lies. And then we lie awake trying to remember whom we told what to so we can keep our stories straight.

The criteria listed in the American Psychiatric Association's DSM-IV for diagnosing alcohol and drug dependency are listed below, as are the criteria for alcohol and drug abuse. Remember, the DSM-IV is still separating alcohol and drugs as being different. To keep it simple, I have adapted the criteria below so they apply to alcohol and/or drug dependency and abuse.

DSM-IV Criteria for Alcohol/Drug Dependency

(A) A maladaptive pattern of alcohol and/or drug use, leading to clinically significant impairment or distress, as manifested by three or more of the following occurring at any time in the same twelve-month period:

Need for markedly increased amounts of alcohol and/or drugs to achieve intoxication or desired effect; or markedly diminished effect with continued use of the same amount of alcohol and/or drugs

The characteristic withdrawal syndrome for alcohol and/or drugs; or drinking and/or using drugs (or using a closely related substance) to relieve or avoid withdrawal symptoms

Drinking/using drugs in larger amounts or over a longer period than intended

Persistent desire or one or more unsuccessful efforts to cut down or control drinking and/or drug use

Important social, occupational, or recreational activities given up or reduced because of drinking and/or drug use

A great deal of time spent in activities necessary to obtain, to use, or to recover from the effects of drinking and/or drug use

Continued drinking and/or drug use despite knowledge of having a persistent or recurrent physical or psychological problem that is likely to be caused or exacerbated by drinking and/or drug use

(B) No duration criterion separately specified, but several dependence criteria must occur repeatedly as specified by duration qualifiers associated with criteria (e.g., "persistent" and "continued")

DSM-IV Criteria for Alcohol/Drug Abuse

A maladaptive pattern of drinking and/or drug use, leading to clinically significant impairment or distress, as manifested by at least one of the following occurring within a twelve-month period:

Recurrent use of alcohol and or drugs resulting in a failure to fulfill major role obligations at work, school, or home (e.g., repeated absences or poor work performance related to alcohol and/or drug use; alcohol- and/or drug-related absences, suspensions, or expulsions from school; neglect of children or household)

Recurrent alcohol and/or drug use in situations in which it is physically hazardous (e.g., driving an automobile or operating a machine when impaired by alcohol and/or drug use)

Recurrent alcohol- and/or drug-related legal problems (e.g., arrests for alcohol and/or drug-related disorderly conduct)

Continued alcohol and/or drug use despite having persistent or recurrent social or interpersonal problems caused or exacerbated by the effects of alcohol and/or drugs (e.g., arguments with spouse about consequences of intoxication)

(B) Never met criteria for alcohol and/or drug dependence

To help you or your loved one better understand these criteria, I want to discuss several issues and define a few terms:

(1) Withdrawal: For many years, withdrawal was interpreted as a physical or physiological event that occurred with abrupt cessation or decreasing amounts of the addictive chemical substance. The acute symptoms of anxiety, tremors, seizures, and delirium tremens (DTs) from alcohol withdrawal are an example. The nausea, vomiting, diarrhea, and generalized muscle aches associated with opioid withdrawal provide another example. For many years, it was assumed that marijuana was not an addictive drug because there were no apparent symptoms of physiological or physical withdrawal. Many medical professionals and insurance companies also did not believe that cocaine was truly addictive because of the lack of physical withdrawal signs. It is true that withdrawal from alcohol, benzodiazepines (Xanax, Valium), and barbiturates (Fiorinal, Phenobarbital) can be life threatening. Many people have died from the hypertension, seizures, and delirium tremens brought on by abruptly stopping or reducing the amount of these substances.

Fortunately, we have learned a great deal about withdrawal and how to treat it. We now understand not only the intensity of withdrawal but also how long it takes. I often say it is very easy to give opinions of withdrawal if you are not the person going through it. The duration of withdrawal from a chemical depends on its fat solubility, or the chemical's ability to be dissolved in fats or oil. It is a well-known fact that some chemicals dissolve more readily in water while some dissolve more readily in oil. To understand this, you may know that water and gasoline do not mix. Pour water into gasoline and you have globs of water floating in the gasoline. Add oil to gasoline, and it mixes together easily. Another example that is not common knowledge is that water added to liquor mixes very nicely. Of course, any decrease in the coloration might be noticed, but no change appears in the consistency.

Why is this important? Benzodiazepines and marijuana have a high fat solubility number, meaning they will take much longer to clear from the body, which consists mostly of water. Marijuana is a very deceptive drug in that I see many patients who say that they have no problem stopping marijuana for days or weeks. Of course, they can quit because their fat is saturated with this drug. I've often said in lectures that this person is a walking marijuana capsule. If you talk to the individual several weeks down the road, you will see someone who is likely very anxious, having insomnia, and displaying irritability that is off the charts. The quick solution to end this discomfort? Smoke more pot. I was pleased to see that the idea of marijuana withdrawal was included in the latest diagnostic manual, DSM-V, in 2013.

Opioids include a wide range of chemicals, such as hydrocodone, oxycodone, and synthetic chemicals, including buprenorphine, butorphanol, and so on. Today, addiction to opioid medications, often by prescription, is the most rapidly growing addiction in our society. I will talk more about this later, but the important point here is that, while fat solubility of these drugs varies widely, the entire class of drugs is highly fat-soluble. Thus, the withdrawal period from these drugs persists for a long time. The acute withdrawal, better known as detoxification, will last for five to seven days — and more — for the long half-life chemicals, such as buprenorphine and methadone. After detoxification, a prolonged withdrawal persists for months, during which time the usual symptoms are depression, anxiety, insomnia, and lack of energy. These symptoms can last anywhere from three to nine months. That duration is one reason why the relapse rate is so high for opioid addicts. For many years, these patients were sent to thirty-day treatment programs, and no one really understood why the relapse rate was so high. Now we know.

Please realize that multiple factors play a role in withdrawal. Many of these will be covered later. What I hope you will remember is that withdrawal is much more than physical. It persists much longer than most people anticipate. In most cases, it is the prolonged withdrawal that is more difficult. So to assume that someone does not qualify for the criteria of withdrawal because they did not have overt physical problems is a mistake. I often ask patients about their quality of life after they have stopped using a chemical. I am assuming they are not using another drug to "compensate." Most will describe it as intolerable, saying they are irritable and discontent. If so, then criterion number one is met. If you are wondering if withdrawal is a problem for you, ask yourself how your quality of your life is when you are using.

(2) Tolerance: This literally means that, over time, it takes more of the chemical to achieve the same effect. I have often heard patients state that one year ago they were taking one or two Vicodin per day but now they are taking thirty every day. Surprisingly, even that dose can become ineffective. They have developed a tolerance to the chemical.

The opposite of that, reverse tolerance, can also occur. The best example is in the person using alcohol. Let me explain. The liver is the organ that metabolizes or breaks down alcohol. Alcohol is the most toxic of the mood-altering drugs, excluding inhalants. Alcohol denatures, or destroys, protein. Human cell membranes are made up of protein, all of them. If you drop a human cell into a

39

vial of alcohol, it will die as the cell wall dissolves. This is why alcohol makes a good antiseptic or disinfectant. Ingested alcohol over time causes generalized damage to the body.

The more active organs, such as the liver and brain, have more damage. So as the liver cells are destroyed, a point is reached in which there are not enough cells available to metabolize alcohol. As this continues, the individual may take in less alcohol. This can be very deceiving. A family member might think the person is doing better, but this reverse tolerance actually is a bad sign! I have had patients sitting in front of me with swollen abdomens (ascites), mental confusion, and skin the color of a lemon (jaundice) trying to impress me (and themselves) that they are now drinking half the quantity of alcohol that they were consuming one year earlier.

Opioid tolerance is also very disturbing. The amount the addict takes slowly increases over time and, as it does, the blood level becomes closer and closer to the lethal dose. This deadly dose varies from person-to-person. It also varies if a person is using something else along with the opioid. Alcohol and benzodiazepines added to opioids often create a lethal combination. Overdose with opioids occurs because these drugs depress the respiratory center in the brain. Alcohol and benzodiazepines also depress this part of the brain, creating an additive effect. The person simply stops breathing.

Many of these deaths occur at night — after the individual has gone to sleep. The involuntary aspect of breathing is lost; the individual is not consciously aware of no longer breathing.

Tolerance is somewhat complicated but the important thing to remember is this: Over some period of time that is different from person-to-person, the drugs quit working! The individual has passed a point where he or she is using the chemical(s) to feel good. Early use produced a high or euphoria. Later, the person

40

would "feel normal" only when using. Ultimately, when feeling normal was not achievable, the person turned to the substance to avoid feeling bad or experiencing withdrawal.

At this point, when the chemicals are no longer working, most individuals are more receptive to treatment and sobriety. A normal person cannot comprehend why addicts behave as they do during these stages. This can be very deceptive to family members who have watched their loved one move from "partying" to more "normal" behavior for a time. The most common statement family members make is, "Oh, they are doing so much better now."

(3) Attempts to stop using are ineffective. At some point in the chemically dependent person's life, he or she will inevitably suspect there might be a problem. Sometimes, that realization is very subtle, almost unconscious, and at other times, the consequences are so great and numerous that a person would have to be unconscious to not see the math in this equation. Attempts are made to quit, but addicts keep those efforts close to the vest. We don't let our families or friends know because, for God's sake, why would we want to be accountable to someone else.

Any addicted person can quit for periods of time, but the problem is staying quit. These time periods can range from days to years. But do not forget that you cannot trust how much time the person claims to have been sober. Again, we (addicts) have a strong tendency to lie about this little issue. I have seen many patients who are proud that they have not used alcohol in X number of months. They will often "forget" to tell you their idea of being sober is using benzodiazepines and smoking THC. They have simply substituted one chemical for another. When we promise our family or friends that we are going to stop using, only to discover we cannot, we often go "underground." The dishonesty becomes more complex, and hiding

41

the chemicals is fascinating to behold. I have often said in lectures that the chemically dependent person is far more creative than most people.

For example, twenty-seven years ago I had a patient who came into the hospital unable to walk because of alcohol damage to the cerebellum. He was hallucinating and damn near dead. After a couple of days, he had cleared mentally, and I asked him if he ever hid his alcohol. I was still fairly new in this field. He said no, and I was baffled because that did not add up. He went on to tell me how his wife was constantly pouring out the vodka bottles, and I asked how he could keep up his usual one liter of vodka intake with this seemingly minor impediment.

"Well, I started putting the vodka in my windshield wiper container and I diverted the hose from the windshield through the firewall in the dashboard. So here was this tube hanging under the steering wheel, and when you turned the windshield wiper switch, bingo! You have vodka." I assure you this is true; I was in awe of the creativity of this gentleman. Even so, I found it necessary to point out to him that normal people do not hide vodka in their windshield washer container. He had convinced himself that this was not an attempt to hide his alcohol; it was merely to beat the challenge of his wife pouring out the vodka.

(4) The term "inability to control the use" includes the inability to stay quit. The loss of control renders the individual unable to predict how much they might use at any given time. For example, a person may say he can go out and have a glass of wine with the family on certain occasions, but, sooner or later, the individual will lose control of his intake and often cannot tell you how much he has consumed. Frequently, such individuals go into a blackout (amnesia) and cannot recall their behavior. They may act in ways that are completely unlike their normal behavior, triggering legal and personal consequences. This phenomenon can and will occur with the other drugs they previously abused but have now returned to using.

42

Alcohol use may not trigger such dramatic events, but, invariably, the person quickly returns to a previous level of use, and the progression continues.

Some addicts may drink or use cocaine only three or four times a year, but when they do, they quickly lose control, resulting in unpleasant consequences. This is called binge using, and over time, the binges become more frequent and last longer. Remember, the diagnosis of chemical dependency is not based on volume, duration, frequency, or what type of chemical the person is using. It is the response that matters. There is absolutely no way you can diagnose a person as an alcoholic just because she drinks every day. Nor can you diagnose her as an addict because she may use cocaine or even heroin. This fact often disturbs many people, especially worried family members. It may sound like an oversimplification but it is true. Chemical dependency occurs when an individual continues to use a mood-altering drug, despite facing unpleasant consequences. This describes chemical dependency in a nutshell.

But there is one problem, which is arguable: The term "consequences" is subjective. For some people, prison is the ultimate consequence. For others, it may be the threatened loss of a marriage — or a job. Because individuals have a different pain tolerance for "consequences," it is not the final consequence that is most important. A great many repercussions before the grand finale have been rationalized away or obliterated by denial. You may assume that most chemically dependent people experience consequences because of what they do. I will tell you that most of the bad outcomes, especially the most painful ones, are because of what the individual does not do. I have talked with many patients who seemed almost proud of the numbers of arrests and job losses they had. When I ask how they feel about the impact on their children and loved ones, the pain of considering the toll was almost unbearable for them. So consequences also occur because of the things we fail to do.

(5) The time consumed in acquiring the chemical, using it, and getting over its effects results in social isolation, decreased job productivity, and losing interest in hobbies and activities that once were enjoyable.

Most normal people do not realize this, but it takes a lot of time and effort to be an alcoholic or addict. For example, as tolerance increases with opioid dependency from one or two Vicodin per day to forty or fifty pills per day (which is not unusual), it takes a great deal of time and ingenuity to find one thousand five hundred Vicodin in a month versus thirty or sixty. Obviously, the cost is much greater, too. To accomplish this, one has to usually find a number of sources that may include multiple doctors. The energy involved becomes much greater because you need to keep your stories straight and keep all of this a secret in many cases. Most people also do not realize that most drug dealers are not very reliable people. You can wait hours or days for them to show up or call, while your desperation escalates. You may have to miss work if you run out or you may have to leave work to obtain your supply because most drug dealers don't have a regular schedule.

The amount of time spent with our loved ones decreases and the quality of our time diminishes because of the unpredictability of whether we may be in withdrawal. So, physically and emotionally, we are separating ourselves from our loved ones. This isolation is inevitable. Some individuals may end up in a dark room with the phone unplugged and tinfoil over the windows. Most, however, experience this gradual movement of separating from a former life to one that is dominated by acquiring the chemical and hanging out with people who use like we do. Chances are, if we are invited over to the preacher's house on Saturday evening for coffee and cookies, we will not choose to go.

For years, our society taught us that it is unlikely for addicts and alcoholics to have or hold onto a job. Because the illness varies from one person to the next, some of

44

these addicts may be our doctors, lawyers, or leaders in our government or military. Many patients come to my office and are proud of the fact that they have never lost a job. Having a steady job, especially a good one, is one of the biggest barriers alcoholics or addicts face in being able to truly see the severity of their disease. Some insist that they do not have a problem, pointing out that they have never missed a day of work and always receive outstanding reviews from their supervisors.

The job is usually the last thing to go in the disease progression. The most common reason, of course, is the job is how we provide for our families and ourselves, including producing the money to continue our alcohol or drug use. Sadly, an even bigger reason is that our job is usually our last source of self-esteem. In our world, so much emphasis is placed on how much money we make. A decent salary is considered a sign we are doing OK. Most chemically dependent individuals do not use alcohol or drugs in the workplace. That may change as the disease progresses, but a drop in productivity occurs long before use on the job. Physicians, although many of them might disagree, are just human beings who happen to have a job practicing medicine. When it comes to this disease, they are no different. Many appear to function for long periods of time.

Dr. Doug Talbot, the past director of an Atlanta-based treatment program that specialized in treating alcoholic and drug-addicted physicians, once said that by the time drug or alcohol use occurred on the job site, the disease had been active and creating consequences in other areas of life for at least seven years. This really is no surprise and is true for all who have this chronic disease. Jobs and work ethic are important but eventually, they, too, fall to this disease.

Another important thing that occurs in this disease process is that hobbies and recreational activities vaporize over time, as do the relationships connected to

45

those activities. Aside from the time spent acquiring the chemical(s), the greatest priority in the addicted person's life is using. It is also likely that the individual has reached a point in the disease where pleasure no longer exists. As a result, the best that one can achieve is to use to not feel bad. This point is important because it has long been known that having fun (or being able to have fun) is a necessary piece of the recovery process. Recovery must be enjoyable, and, if it isn't, then it is not likely the individual will stay sober.

During my first week of treatment in 1985, the counselor called a meeting on a Friday afternoon and announced that the "event" for this particular night was called Forced Fun. Try and picture this: Here are forty-five or so drug addicts and alcoholics, all in some stage of withdrawal or detoxification. They were doctors, lawyers, bikers, and people of all ages. We were told a bus would pick us up and that after this "event," we would have a short group session. The bus took our motley crew to a nearby putt-putt golf facility where we unloaded. We watched as the counselors got back on the bus and said they hoped we would have a good time. Suddenly, we realized that no one else was playing there. Several patients wondered aloud if we had scared off everybody. What we were supposed to do now?

Most of us stood around and were at a loss. Others smoked cigarettes and gathered in groups of three or four. God only knows what the topic of conversation was. A few scaled the fence to go to the nearby Kroger store for God knows what. It was a muggy, hot, miserable two hours. When we returned to the facility, the counselors asked what we had learned. I recall going into this long diatribe, complaining that we were paying a great deal of money to this place, and that the purpose of the event, I surmised, was to give the counselors a couple of extra hours to work on their charts. I had many supporters chiming in. When we finally quieted down, the counselor simply said, "You don't know how to have fun anymore, do you?" That was an immediate buzz kill. Not one person in the room could argue that point.

46

(6) The last of the criteria is very complex, but simply put: The person keeps using despite knowledge of having a persistent physical or psychological problem caused or worsened by the substance use. Again, the criteria are wonderful but the words "knowledge of having a problem" are something that I believe every alcoholic and addict would argue with. Now, these criteria were written by a group of normal human beings, most likely. I seriously doubt they consulted a group of alcoholics and addicts to help them fine-tune this one. In my experience, it has been rare that a person comes to me with knowledge that alcohol or drugs are causing physical or emotional damage. Perhaps very late in the disease a few people will reach that conclusion.

The vast majority of patients report that the reason they use alcohol and drugs is because of their emotional or physical problems. Denial, rationalization, blaming, and so on are the psychological mechanisms that prevent most chemically dependent individuals from realizing what has damaged them. There has been a great deal of debate in the medical field about what causes addiction. Is the mental illness primary, or is it the chemical use that is causing mental illness symptoms? For many years, professionals in the field of addiction medicine believed that the vast majority of patients would be normal if they stopped using alcohol or drugs. That viewpoint was wrong, and it is likely that many patients relapsed because they had an untreated psychiatric diagnosis.

On the flip side, during the 1980s and '90s, a large group of professionals believed that if the psychiatric problem was properly treated, the individual would not need to drink or drug. Both camps were wrong. I hope today we have moved to the point where patients are considered individuals with backgrounds, genes, and experiences that are unique. Certainly, a high percentage of individuals have a coexisting psychiatric disorder. The term "coexisting" is very important because someone may begin using alcohol or drugs as a way to cope with the discomfort

47

caused by a psychiatric illness, but they continue to use because they also have a chemical dependency disease.

In many cases, an individual with a coexisting psychiatric disorder can usually be identified. A strong family history of psychiatric disorders in relatives who did not have addictions is one clue. Also, if the patient exhibited symptoms of a psychiatric illness before using mood-altering drugs, this is another sign a true psychiatric disorder may coexist. This sounds fairly simple, and, to some degree, it is. What can be overlooked, though, is whether this individual is married to an alcoholic or drug addict. Or, did the person grow up in a family in which mom or dad was alcoholic and/or drug addicted? Those circumstances change a person.

If you are wondering about yourself, take an honest look at your life. You might need a trusted friend to help you. See if any of these describes your behavior:

1. You continue to use alcohol or drugs, despite troubling consequences. For example, drinking while on probation for a DWI should be an eye opener.

2. You can't stop using all mood-altering chemicals completely for at least a year.

3. The fear of withdrawing is so overwhelming that quitting is incomprehensible to you.

4. Your social circle has diminished to the point that you only hang out with people who drink or drug as you do.

5. You hide your chemicals and sometimes even forget where you put them.

6. You find yourself repeatedly lying about your chemical use, where you have been, and other behaviors. You lie so much you have trouble remembering what you told to whom.

7. When you are not using, you exist in a state of restlessness, irritability, and discontentment.

8. You cannot imagine living without more chemicals.

9. You have no spiritual connection or hope. You don't care whether you live or die.

10. The alcohol and drugs are no longer working (except for that fleeting nanosecond when you first use), and the best you can hope for is that you don't have a bad day.

A yes to any of these statements indicates a tremendous probability that you have the disease of chemical dependency.

The good news is: You have a disease that is treatable. While it is true that we all have a choice in the beginning on whether to use alcohol or drugs, having this disease does not make you a bad person. I have never yet heard a patient say that when mom or dad asked what he or she wanted to become as a grown-up, the person's goal was to be a junkie or a drunk. Never!

As I mentioned, the criteria for alcohol and drug dependency are the same. The criteria for alcohol and drug abuse are important. But everyone with this disease passes through the abuse stage very quickly, maybe in the first week of using. The difference is, substance abusers can stop or change their chemical use and avoid the multiple consequences that bedevil addicts.

As we learn more about this disease, perhaps someday there will be medical approaches that arrest or prevent chemical dependency. In the past few decades, medications have been used to help move an individual towards sobriety. They are only helpful, though, if that person truly wants to get clean and sober. Without that desire, these medications are useless. It is important to realize that only about 5 percent of people who have this disease will have even a chance to receive formal treatment. Millions have died and more will follow them because they do not know their disease is treatable. Society programmed them to believe something was

49

wrong or defective about them. Doctor after doctor failed to tell them that there was hope and that remission was possible. These doctors were not trained adequately about a disease that affects one out of every ten patients they see. As young physicians, they were teachable and enthusiastic, but the opportunity was missed. Now, they are like most people in our society, exhibiting little empathy and mostly anger towards this "defective" group of people.

In general, training physicians already practicing in the real world is ineffective. The physician has already developed his or her own ideas about alcohol and drug addiction. If our medical institutions would teach the students about chemical dependency equal to the training they receive for treating diabetes, hypertension, and cardiovascular disease, then perhaps the epidemic that is destroying our society could be contained.

I hope our criminal justice system could in some way provide training to those entering the legal profession. Our criminal justice system is choked with individuals who are not sociopaths, murderers, or deviants, but who commit crimes because of their disease. This does not mean that addiction is an excuse for their criminal behavior. But if we could recognize the disease and provide treatment for those who are willing to do the work necessary to stay sober, it is unlikely they will reenter the revolving door of the criminal justice system. Punishment by itself has never worked. Just look at the millions of young (and old) men and women who have criminal records that prevent them from obtaining housing or a job. Without treatment and hope, these circumstances are not likely to change.

Alcohol is the most physically destructive mood altering drug that exists.

Chapter 5: Physical Consequences of Chemical Use

The physical consequences, while often scary, are not sufficient by themselves to stop the person from continuing to use. Any attempt to use fear usually will not work. What is truly amazing, though, is that once addicts start the recovery process, one of their biggest concerns is the state of their health, especially the condition of their liver. It is also common to see patients refuse other medications because of their concern that these prescribed chemicals might cause liver damage!

Before going into the specifics, I want to make clear that other than the inhalants (gasoline, Freon, etc.), alcohol is the most physically destructive mood-altering drug that exists. Oddly, most people are surprised when they hear this, probably because alcohol is a legal drug and generally accepted in our society. Yet, alcohol is more toxic than heroin, cocaine, THC, or methamphetamine. The other drugs I mentioned have their specific dangers, and I will discuss those later.

Alcohol alters the structure of a protein, breaking many of its bonds, a process called denaturation. The damage to the body is generally very slow and subtle. Binge drinking, common in our young people today, is also dangerous because of the rapid rise and higher blood alcohol levels that are achieved. Consequences of binge drinking in the short-term are related more to alcohol poisoning.

The human body is an incredibly durable structure. I have said many times that God must have considered alcoholics when he designed the liver because it has the capacity to regenerate itself. We also have a great deal of extra liver tissue "just in case." I deeply respect the concerns that patients express about their livers. In the vast majority of cases, I can assure them that they will be fine, provided they stop drinking. For some, however, the line has been crossed, and the likelihood their liver can return to normal functioning is not possible. It often has been reported that women experience more damage, drink-for-drink, than men. This is true. A significant number of women have a genetic deficiency that does not allow their bodies to produce adequate amounts of an enzyme called alcohol dehydrogenase. This results in higher blood alcohol levels, which cause more damage. Below is the simple metabolism of alcohol:

(1) Alcohol >alcohol dehydrogenase > Acetaldehyde

(2) Acetaldehyde> acetaldehyde dehydrogenase > CO_2, H_2O, Acetic Acid

The "flow" of the equation is held up at the first step when the liver is damaged. Alcohol is a very simple molecule and so is its metabolism. For those individuals who progress on to cirrhosis and continue to drink, death is slow. Although there probably is no good way to die, this really is a bad way to exit the planet. Lethargy, confusion, gastrointestinal bleeding, seizures, and coma often characterize death by cirrhosis.

The next major category of chemicals includes cocaine and methamphetamine. There are a number of stimulants; some are synthetic and most are derivatives of the amphetamine molecule. The consequences of these drugs are from the vasoconstrictive effects of this chemical. This means an artery will constrict or shrink in size, reducing its diameter and restricting blood flow to an organ. This decrease in blood flow can result in a heart attack or a stroke. It is logical that older individuals who have smaller arterial openings from atherosclerosis will have a higher chance of such consequences.

No one can predict when this might happen. I have a patient who had been addicted to cocaine for several years but had achieved a rather long period of sobriety (four or five years). Then, she met some old friends, used a small amount of cocaine, and had a myocardial infarction (heart attack). She was middle-aged, healthy, and, fortunately, survived. She was totally baffled by the event but ended up learning a great deal. She now understood the danger of hanging out with old friends who still used — and the never-ending potential for consequences

The consequences of using cocaine and mixing it with alcohol, which seems to be the norm today, can be fatal. The combination produces a substance called cocaethylene. It causes irritability of the heart, and heart attacks can even occur in people who do not have narrowing of the arteries. Death can occur abruptly.

Another significant point about cocaine is that use over time can produce what is called the "kindling effect." This means that the probability of having a grand mal seizure gets greater over time. Most people think of a seizure as an event that occurs with withdrawal. In this case, it is the opposite! There is much more to know and understand about these chemicals and their impact.

Opioids are in a general class of drugs that have a large number of specific molecules. The more commonly known varieties of these painkillers are Vicodin (hydrocodone), Percodan and OxyContin (oxycodone), Demerol, Dilaudid, Methadone, and Codeine. Additionally, there are the synthetic opioids, such as Stadol, Nubain, Suboxone, and Darvon. Fentanyl is a very potent and quick acting opioid. Recently street drugs such as heroin, has had fentanyl added. That combination has resulted in a greater number of overdoses. The amount of deadly fentanyl is 100 times less than heroin and addicts often don't realize that the heroin they just bought has been laced with fentanyl The dependence on prescription opioids is the most rapidly increasing type of addiction in our society today! This bears repeating because this epidemic is unlikely to decrease unless the medical profession stops contributing to the supply.

One of the first points to remember about opioids is that even those people who do not have the disease of addiction can become physically dependent on these chemicals. Several years ago, a respected attorney came to my office. She had been seeing a physician who had been prescribing 240 milligrams of OxyContin per day for her migraine headaches. She had no family history of chemical dependency and reported no personal history of abusing alcohol or drugs. She came to see me because every time she tried to stop this medication, or ran out of pills, she became violently ill.

She experienced vomiting, diarrhea, chills, and muscle cramps for days. Of course, a migraine headache usually appeared at some point. She had not been buying drugs off the street and she had never taken more than the prescribed dose. She was not hiding her pills or lying about her use. She was not missing work, and no one had expressed any concern about her ability to practice law. I considered her physically dependent and believed it unlikely that she had the disease of addiction. Yet she was experiencing the same withdrawal symptoms that would occur in the opioid (chemically dependent) addict. If she could successfully get off of this medication, it was unlikely that she would ever return to it. Her prognosis was good.

She still would need to address her migraines but in a way that would not cause dependence on opioids. Using opioids for migraines often causes a rebound of the headaches, increasing the potential for dependency.

Withdrawal from opioids is, without a doubt, the most painful and miserable form of withdrawal. It is unlikely that anyone will die from opioid withdrawal, but I assure you that you feel like you are going to. The fear of withdrawal is a major force in maintaining the addiction. As I mentioned earlier, it is likely that even at high doses the individual is not experiencing euphoria or pleasure any longer. The person is only trying to stay out of withdrawal. This may be hard to imagine, but perhaps it will offer some insight if I tell you that patients often say, "Even my hair was hurting." The intensity of the pain from opioid withdrawal sometimes prevents even the non-chemically dependent person from quitting. I will discuss this more when we talk about sobriety.

In the United States, opioid overdoses exceed the number of vehicle fatalities. I have written earlier about why people die from drugs. Mixing opioids with alcohol, benzodiazepines, or other sedatives is a cocktail for death. Period.

Now let's look at marijuana. This chemical primarily causes damage to the lungs because it typically is smoked. Years ago, there were stories about the great damaging effects of THC. Remember the old scare film, Reefer Madness? Again, fear did not stop most people from using. The fact is, smoking one joint equals smoking about six cigarettes. It is logical that smoking something without a filter delivers more particulate matter to the lungs and, thus, causes more damage. There is no question that smoking pot can lead to COPD (chronic obstructive pulmonary disease).

The benzodiazepines and other sedatives are classified as anti-anxiety meds and hypnotics. A tremendous number of people have a severe addiction to these chemicals, and many of them, similar to opioid users, become physically dependent. Any person who takes a therapeutic or normally prescribed dose of benzodiazepines (i.e., five milligrams of Valium twice a day) for more than forty-five days will experience withdrawal. It comes in the form of anxiety, which is fascinating because that is the problem the drug was prescribed to treat in the first place. Even worse, the anxiety during withdrawal usually is magnified. In other words, long-term use results in a condition that may seem to require more of the same medication.

The withdrawal from a drug is the opposite of the effect of the drug. This has been known for a long time in the medical profession. Yet it still is common to see physicians prescribe medication improperly. When Valium came on the market in 1963, physicians were told that it was not an addictive drug. We now know that Valium is addictive as are all of its derivatives, including Xanax, Ativan, and Klonopin.

The benzodiazepine drug itself is not toxic to the body. But one of the dangers of this class of medication is that, as tolerance occurs and dosages increase, a fatal blood level can be reached. Like the opioids, this dose varies from person-to-person. Benzodiazepines depress respiration as do the opioids — but not to the same degree. We seldom see pure benzodiazepine overdoses, but when combined with another central nervous system depressant, such as alcohol or opioids, fatal overdoses are common. These substances also cause a profound loss of short-term memory.

Abruptly stopping a benzodiazepine — or dramatically decreasing the dosage — can result in a grand mal or epileptic seizure. These can be fatal. It takes several months of use to create this type of complication, but because there is a great deal of variability in who will have a seizure, one must never abruptly stop these medications.

Part of this group of drugs includes the barbiturates (Phenobarbital, Nembutal, Seconal) and the non-barbiturate sedative hypnotics. Barbiturates are seldom prescribed today but are still useful in preventing seizures.

Many other hypnotics are on the market, but one of particular importance is Zolpidem, commonly known as Ambien. Most medical professionals have considered it a non-addictive drug, but it definitely is habit-forming! I recently had a physician come into my office who was taking up to 150 milligrams of Ambien per day. That is fifteen times the average dose. Another peculiarity about Ambien is the amnesia that occurs in many people, even those who are not chemically dependent. That can create a dangerous situation because this amnesia is similar to an alcohol blackout. The individual may suddenly come out of the amnesia and realize he or she is driving a car with no recollection of how this happened.

Because Ambien attaches adjacent to the benzodiazepine receptor, individuals who are in recovery should not take this medication. Alternatives to Ambien exist, but many insurance companies refuse to cover them and pressure physicians to prescribe Ambien because it is less expensive.

Another group of chemicals deserving attention are referred to as "designer drugs." The designer drugs have been around since the appearance of Ecstasy, patented in 1914 as MDMA. It initially was used in psychiatry then faded into obscurity until the 1980s, when it re-emerged as Ecstasy. It was widely used in the open until 1985, when it became illegal.

A designer drug is one that has been altered by either adding or deleting atom(s) from the original molecule. It is more complicated than that, but, basically, the original drug's structure is changed, allowing an illegal drug to become legal. That is because our laws are very specific about a drug's chemical structure. Government action is needed to ban the drug.

Some chemists have managed to stay ahead of the changing laws, and today, the number of designer drugs is amazing. These chemists hope to maintain the mood-altering quality of the drug while increasing its potency. But even small molecular changes can cause devastating medical problems for test subjects, often drug addicts. I am certain these drugs did not meet the rigorous standards for U.S. Food and Drug Administration (FDA) approval. Many people have died, suffered neurological damage, or developed a permanent psychosis. Not all of the consequences are known.

Designer drugs, however, remain prevalent. Many are sold in stores, such as head shops, derived from marijuana or amphetamine molecules. It is difficult to keep up with the slang terminology, but Spice and bath salts are two common street names. The molecules of Spice are similar to those of marijuana, and bath salts are similar to the molecules of amphetamines.

The problems occur because the user's response is not predictable. The side effects are also unknown and can be long-term, if not permanent.

For example, a twenty-year-old college student came to the office. He had been using marijuana and alcohol for the past three years and had been functioning well without any major consequences. He was preparing to enter his junior year in college when he decided to smoke Spice. Within three hours, he became disoriented, paranoid, and lost touch with reality. Over the next forty-eight hours, his symptoms lessened, but he was not able to attend class or comprehend the instructional material. I saw this young man several more times, and his symptoms did improve. He might have been forever changed by his one and only encounter with Spice. Hopefully, his symptoms will disappear over the years, but we cannot predict the outcome. These drugs are mood-altering and dangerous.

The last example I will mention is of a patient in his early fifties. I had seen this man for several years, and he was sober. A few months ago, I received information that he had been hospitalized for a stroke. He admitted using bath salts immediately before experiencing the stroke. I have not seen him since and sincerely hope he has recovered. Using any designer drug is dangerous, and I strongly advise people to stay away from them. It does not matter whether they are legal.

The last group of chemicals I want to discuss are the hallucinogens, a class in which the federal government has oddly placed marijuana. Generally speaking, we are referring to LSD, psilocybin (mushrooms), and peyote (a small spineless cactus). The half-lives of these drugs are variable, and they can vary from one person to the next. The half-life is the time it takes the body to clear half of the drug, and that time can depend on how big or little someone is. The quantity necessary to cause hallucinations is small. We do not see people who are truly addicted to these drugs. I guess you don't find people who enjoy hallucinating all of the time. There is little to no tolerance.

The danger is some people will develop a psychosis (out of touch with reality) that does not go away. In medicine today, we think that these individuals are likely predisposed to having a mental illness that had not been evident before the use of the hallucinogen. Often, there is a family history of mental illness in these individuals. Almost everyone has heard about deaths brought on by using hallucinogens. Sadly, LSD is making a comeback and is now prevalent among teens.

Now, considering all of these classes of chemicals, let's look at how they work in the brain and what makes them addictive. The last part of this explanation will be understood by anyone who has this disease. For those who do not, it may be the closest you will ever come to understanding what happens in the dependent brain.

The mesolimbic brain, also known as the survival brain, consists of the nucleus accumbens, the pleasure center. It is also the center for propagation of the species, fight-or-flight, thirst, and hunger. It's a little more complicated than this anatomically, but for ease of understanding, this part of the brain holds an incredibly powerful cluster of neurons that function subconsciously. One way to think about the effect of chemicals in this area is to consider how some chemicals stimulate the hunger center (marijuana), and some depress it, like cocaine. Cocaine also causes hypersexuality in some people while in others, it stimulates the fight-or-flight center. Many drugs affect the thirst center and so on. Thirst and hunger are the most powerful urges that contribute to survival. The most dangerous human being is the person who is thirsty or hungry. Many of you have read accounts of cannibalism, most recently reported in refugees from Vietnam who were stranded at sea. In an average day, most of us don't really think about how thirsty or hungry we are. We just stop at the water fountain or eat often enough to prevent excessive hunger. Most of us have never experienced hunger or thirst that was life-threatening.

This very thing is happening in the addicted brain. This "need" for the chemical is really no different than the need someone might have for food and water. As a person gets thirstier and hungrier, the addict gets more dysphoric, or uncomfortable.

What is happening is a portion of the brain (the survival brain) is announcing that the body needs something. This is why many alcoholics or addicts do not have really good reasons why they use. As time elapses, the brain becomes desperate for alcohol and/or drugs, and the message gets louder and louder. The brain tells the person he or she will die if the craving is not satisfied immediately: Do drugs now

Never, ever tell friends or loved ones they are an alcoholic
or an addict.

Chapter 6: How to Identify the Chemically Dependent Person

Drug use does not necessarily mean that the person is an alcoholic or drug addict. The diagnosis is not based on volume, duration, frequency, or type of chemical. I would not urge anyone reading this to go out and start diagnosing your family members or friends. They do not like it.

The idea for this chapter came from my work with family medicine residents several years ago. They had one week at our treatment facility as part of their psychiatric rotation. Believe me, one week provides little time for an education. I had to decide what I could do to help these residents so they could one day help their own patients.

I thought that the best place to start was by teaching them how to identify the chemically dependent patient. I had no hope that I could help them really understand the disease or know how to treat it. They all had the latest Diagnostic and Statistical Manual for Mental Disorders in their pockets, but putting the criteria into the real world of the patient did not make sense. So this is what I did.

The first thing I told them was about the powerful tendency for alcoholics and addicts to lie to them. You cannot believe much of anything that they tell you, I said. The looks of surprise on their faces were truly a Kodak moment. The room was silent for quite some time.

I then talked about the "art of medicine," when a physician senses that something is wrong and is not deterred by the information provided by the patient. I went on to explain that while some of this was dishonesty, the forces of denial and rationalization were so strong in these individuals that they believed their own story. They often are convincing. I then pointed out that one out of ten patients has this disease. So awareness was of utmost importance. None of the residents had any idea of what to say to a patient if they suspected alcohol or drug addiction. I went on to tell them that chemical dependency is a chronic, progressive disease, meaning they should approach an addicted patient the same way they would a diabetic or someone with cardiovascular disease. An index of suspicion is usually the first step. Next comes the gathering of more information to confirm the diagnosis. I pointed out that it would be unlikely that they could complete a diagnosis on the chemically dependent patient in one session.

The first approach I suggested was the same tactic I have advised to family members and friends over the years. The most simple, non-threatening, and nonjudgmental way is to say, "I am concerned that you may have a problem with alcohol or drugs." Never, ever tell friends or loved ones they are an alcoholic or an addict. It is very difficult, though, for anyone to argue with the word "concern." Next, it is important to acknowledge that if indeed there is a problem, alcoholism or drug addiction is a disease, and help is available. No one can predict how the person will respond, but avoid provoking anger. I guarantee that will be the response if the person trying to help accuses the individual of being an alcoholic or addict. I advised the residents to not expect anything from this meeting but to look at it as an opportunity to "plant the seed." Once a true alcoholic or addict hears what you have told them, they never forget it. Sometimes, it will take months, or perhaps years, for that patient to return seeking help, but the door has been opened.

Please realize that most of these statements are generalizations, but if the equation adds up, you will be in the right ballpark. I advised the physicians that being in family practice put them in a unique position to really get to know their patients and to help. They will notice if a patient is acting differently or if the person's appearance changes. For reasons I do not understand, addiction medicine literature does not discuss this red flag. In most individuals who are in the early stages of their disease, especially teenagers, fairly dramatic changes emerge in their attitudes, the friends they hang out with, sleeping patterns, eating, socializing with family, and even their grooming. One of the most common things I have seen over the years is the young person who has been very active in sports will suddenly quit. Perhaps the person has a legitimate reason for quitting, but it is such a common occurrence in chemically dependent youth that I believe it should be noted. Emotionally, the young person becomes defiant and argumentative. Although these points are not diagnostic of chemical dependency, they suggest the onset of drug use. Add to this a strong family history of alcohol and drug dependency, and you can see that the young person's problems are just beginning. Parents need to pay attention to these changes as well.

As for physical changes to notice, almost everyone knows the smell of alcohol and THC. Yet most alcoholics don't appear drunk, and most drug addicts do not stumble around or nod off. This may sound odd to some people, but I suggested to the residents that they look at their patients' eyes. Of course, very big pupils suggest stimulant use, and tiny, pinpoint pupils suggest opioid use, although other things can cause pupil changes.

I believe in the adage that "the eyes are the windows to soul." Some people will notice that the person's eyes have a glassy appearance, and a look of "disconnection." If you know that person, you will see it. Do not ignore this; there may or may not be any other signs. I have had the opportunity to meet with thousands of alcoholics and addicts over the years. On one occasion many years ago, several physicians and I were meeting with another doctor whom we were concerned about because of troubling reports from patients and colleagues. The physician was quite angry with our group and he loudly protested that he did not use drugs and that we had made a big mistake. I had been quiet during this intervention, but I simply said to him, "You are high right now." His eyes gave him away. I have since come to know this doctor and consider him a friend. I have never seen the same look that I saw in his eyes that day and I doubt I ever will again.

Although this is a generalization, I have come to believe that alcoholics and addicts are masters at using anger to protect their disease. Of course, this is mostly subconscious. Most people have trouble dealing with anger, and addicts tap into it easily. Anger is magical in that it also provides a diversionary tactic, a way to switch the conversation to trying to convince you that you are the crazy one. If this has ever happened to you, then you understand what I am talking about.

You can catch an alcoholic drinking out of a bottle or even a drug addict with a needle in his arm, but before you know it, that person has convinced you that what you are seeing is not true and that something must be terribly wrong with you. The odd thing is, you begin to believe it. Other people do not act this way. It is a craft that is honed by addicts. Anger is also effective at manipulating medical professionals. Addicts may use it to get a desired prescription. For some reason, most physicians don't deal very well with a patient's anger, finding it easier to acquiesce.

I briefly touched on the subject of dishonesty when I mentioned training the family medicine residents. We need to talk more about this. Dishonesty is not unique to alcoholics and addicts. We live in a society that accepts and tolerates dishonesty in many ways. Many people are adept at dishonesty by what they don't say (sins of omission). Others are considered to be pathological liars, and most of us know someone like this. Then we have the man who is known for his integrity and fairness, but when he catches a four-pound bass, the fish somehow gets larger over time. By the time the story is shared with his grandchildren, the fish has broken state records. That may sound extreme, but the point is, it hard to find a person who is absolutely honest.

Most alcoholics and addicts fall under the big part of the bell on the bell curve. As their disease progresses, they reach a level of dishonesty that baffles most people, especially the family. This is most noticeable in teenagers, but it is not unique to this group. Initially, addicted individuals will lie about what they are using and how much. You could call this minimization if you would like a better term. Because fueling the addiction takes a lot more time out of their lives, they begin to be dishonest about where they have been and with whom they have been associating. The last part of this sentence is especially important to parents. If your child suddenly quits hanging out with old friends and is now hanging with people who appear to be druggies, guess what? Your child is using drugs. The dishonesty takes on a life of its own, and the alcoholic or drug addict has to lie to cover the tales that have been told. It gets very confusing and I have had hundreds of family members say they really aren't sure what the truth is anymore. They are correct!

Something else that should be a tip-off is the fine art of hiding substances. I briefly mentioned the gentleman who hid his vodka in the windshield-washer container. Normal people do not hide their liquor in the commode tank and they do not keep pints of liquor in the pocket of an old dress coat they have not worn in years. Normal people do not buy fake electrical outlets so they can keep their marijuana or their pills in a safe place. So, friends and family members, if you are finding alcohol and drugs stashed in bizarre places, you have something to be concerned about. Your loved one's use of chemicals is not normal.

Emotional detachment is something else to consider. This withdrawal can occur with mental illnesses, such as depression, so it is not unique to chemically dependent people. As the disease progresses, most alcoholics and addicts tend to avoid family members because you know them all too well. This detachment may come as being too busy with their social life or spending countless hours in their room completely avoiding human contact. It is not uncommon to see someone who is highly successful in the business world who has lost a marriage or two long before their chemical use has become evident in the workplace.

Over the years I have been asked by employers to do presentations on how to identify chemical dependency in the workplace. I often mention that there are certain patterns to look for. One is the individual who misses every Monday because of a stomach virus. This one is fairly easy. Then you have the person who routinely has the three- to five-day illnesses right after every payday. The harder sign to detect is the decreased productivity that occurs slowly over time. I often have said that addicts and alcoholics are some of the best employees out there. Some may be only functioning at 50 percent capacity, but they are still very productive. In time, the disease wins. Thank goodness, many employers have educated themselves about this disease. They have learned that treatment does work and that it is more cost-effective to help an employee than it is to train someone new. They have also learned that the sober employee is dependable, honest, and usually, very appreciative of the employer.

Drug screening is now prevalent in the workplace, and it's a noble cause if it is used to help those who have the disease of chemical dependency. It is also an effective tool to weed out people who may be smoking pot or using heroin. This is the primary reason for pre-employment urine screening. The only problem with random drug screening is that the positive screen is only evidence that a person has used a drug; it does not indicate that the employee is an alcoholic or addict. Fortunately, human resource departments have developed to help determine if treatment is an option for those who test positive.

I believe that the single most important thing family members can do for their loved ones and themselves is attend Al-Anon meetings.

Chapter 7: The Family

Chemical dependency affects the entire family, 100 percent of the time. There are no exceptions. Years ago, little attention was paid to the family members. The focus was on the addicted person, and families would just have to adapt and understand. As time progressed, however, it became clear to those working in the addiction field that this disease had a tremendous effect on family members. Our treatment centers started providing three-to-five-day programs for family members to help them have a better understanding of addiction. Early on, those programs also provided an opportunity for the entire family to sit in a circle and remind their loved one of all the things they had done. This was more of an attempt to break through the addicted person's denial, rather than having any therapeutic value for the family. As we came to understand more about family systems and dynamics, it became increasingly clear that the family's dysfunction was often greater than their loved one's disease. We learned that the addicted person must change to remain sober and that the family members must also change to achieve and maintain a healthier family life.

The best way I can describe this is by sharing an experience I had sometime in the late 1980s. A woman by the name of Pat O'Neil was doing a presentation at one of our local hospitals. Pat walked onto the stage carrying a mobile, but instead of looking like a whimsical plaything, this mobile had figures that represented a mother, father, and two children. I had known Pat for quite some time, but I was wondering what in the hell a mobile had to do with her presentation. Pat said that the laws of nature dictate that every family exists in some type of balance. She said that this balance does not mean the family is healthy; it can and will occur even in the most pathological situations. Her point was this: If you change one person in this system (she demonstrated this by adding weight to one figure), the other

70

members would have to change, too. Indeed, after removing weight from one structure, the mobile did regain a balance, although it was different than the original. This was profound to me because it began to make sense that sobriety was about change for everyone. Without it, the family system would no longer exist.

I believe that the single most important thing family members can do for their loved ones and themselves is attend Al-Anon meetings. I have spent years encouraging this. Still, it is more likely the addicted family member will attend AA or NA (Narcotics Anonymous) meetings than it is for the families to attend Al-Anon. I would estimate that at the end of the first year of treatment, only 2 percent of family members are attending a 12-step program. I have said in many lectures that the denial in family members often meets or exceeds that of the patient. The excuses given by the family are numerous. I've been too busy. I am not the one who needs help. I've been to meetings and all they do is complain. I don't like to talk about our problems. These excuses are very similar to those offered by the patients. I have often sat in mouth-gaping awe listening to family members whose dysfunction made the patient look good by comparison.

Remember, most symptoms of chemical dependency are behavioral; that is why they are included in the Diagnostic and Statistical Manual for Mental Disorders. Over time, as the addicted person's behavior becomes more pathological, the family members begin to adapt so they can understand or explain the behavior that initially seemed so perplexing. These changes take place over time, and that is why they are so hard to see.

Families adjust to problems in many different ways. Some of the accommodating behavior might have been learned in childhood. Perhaps in mom's family, the unspoken rule was to just not talk about any problems. As an example, I grew up in East Texas (Marshall), a part of Texas that has its own unique culture. Anyhow,

71

I was twelve or thirteen when I was attending one of our infamous family reunions. I suddenly saw a man who appeared to be in his fifties. I had never met him, so I asked my mother who he was. She told me he was my Uncle Ross. Well, I had no idea that I had an Uncle Ross. When I asked where he had been, my mother told me he was an alcoholic and had been in prison. She added that I was to keep my mouth shut about it. It turned out for me, of course, that Uncle Ross was the coolest member of the whole family. But I got my mom's hushed message loud and clear: Don't talk about such things, and if you should find out, keep your mouth zipped.

Some families explode when a problem comes up. Utter chaos ensues until a solution is found to "fix" the problem. Dad goes into a rage, and mom starts wailing at the top of her lungs. Things go south from there. This type of family typically believes the solution is for their loved one to "quit that stuff right now." As if that were even possible.

Most destructive of all is the family that communicates in deceptive language. Often these families use guilt as their major weapon. The communication circles around in cryptic terms, and no one is quite sure of the meaning. A typical response in this family is, "Gosh, you look tired." The addict knows damn well what this means, but no one else does. I could go on and on, but my message is that families develop their own adaptive strategies when a loved one is using.

As time progresses and the addict's dishonesty and deceptive behaviors increase, family members are now losing their trust. Unfortunately, no one is willing to admit it. This is a time to put a GPS on their son or daughter's car or make constant phone calls trying to pinpoint what is going on. The parents or spouse may lie awake fearful of what may have happened. Fear slowly takes over their lives. This is usually replaced by anger, and when anger is turned inward or left expressed, it will come out as depression or anxiety. It is not uncommon for family members to start seeking help at this point for their own symptoms. In the case of parents, their marriage begins to fall apart because the focus is again on the child who is the alcoholic or drug addict. Oddly, marriages can falter even if the parents are on the same page. If they have different ideas about how the problem should be handled, the marriage will face even greater challenges.

I mentioned earlier about working with family medicine residents. I emphasized the importance of identifying the family members of alcoholics and addicts because if these doctors did not recognize the common denominator of the family dynamics, then no one was going to get better.

My first experience with seeing the impact on family members occurred in 1986 while I was working in a minor emergency center. I vividly recall it to this day. A woman came in one evening and complained she was having a headache for months. She pointed to the muscles in the back of her neck and described a headache that extended up to the sides of her scalp and over to her shoulder blades. The muscles were in a state of spasm. She denied any other symptoms, other than saying she had trouble sleeping and was often depressed. Her eyes were sadder than any I had seen in quite some time. The anxiety and depression were permeating her life. I had only been sober for a short time and honestly had no clue then how sick family members can get when dealing with an addicted loved one. It was the same look in her eyes that I had seen in my family's eyes that led me ask her, "By chance, is there anyone in your family that has a drinking or drug problem?" I will never forget the sense of relief that filled her eyes when she acknowledged that her husband had a bad drinking problem. She went on to talk about the financial burdens and the behavioral problems that her kids were having in school. I saw this clearly for the first time and I talked to her about the disease of alcoholism and the importance of her going to Al-Anon meetings. She would learn from the experiences of others who had already been in her place. I told her that medicine would not help her neck, and she understood. I never saw her again

73

and I hope life went well for her. She taught me something, though, that I never forgot.

It goes back to what I said earlier about long-held beliefs. Family members believe an addict shoots drugs and an alcoholic is always drunk and can't hold a job. They see their own loved one, but can't figure out why things are so bad. The family often makes excuses for the drug addict or alcoholic because the truth, while still unrecognized, would be too unbearable. Parents call the school to make sure their son or daughter gets an excused absence because they have that intestinal problem again. Spouses call the workplace to give one more excuse because they are terrified their loved one will lose another job.

I want to quickly make a point to parents who are just finding out that their son or daughter is drinking or using drugs. There is no one right way to handle the situation, but here are some points to keep in mind. If you believe for some reason that pot is harmless, you are dead wrong. Orally or even nonverbally supporting the use of marijuana may well lead to a disaster. Although your son or daughter may be telling you that all the kids are doing it, they aren't. Even assuming that every other kid is using, why in God's name would you allow your child to use one of the most toxic drugs that exists? If you have a family history of alcohol or drug addiction and you condone the use of mood-altering drugs in your child, you may have just completed the equation. Genetic Risk + Chemical = Disease.

Let me also clarify that the vast majority of people who use alcohol or even other drugs will never become addicted. Most members of my profession and myself have no issue with someone who chooses to drink or drug. Prohibition did not work, and I assure you that despite the billions spent on preventing drug trafficking, the supply is steady and is not going to stop. For every dealer who is arrested, five more will take his or her place because it's a lucrative business.

Educating our children through various programs, such as D.A.R.E., represent valiant attempts to fight this disease, but education by itself has been ineffective. You may be able to educate the child, but if the parents are not included, the attempt is futile. Also, the idea that a child can be educated enough in a few sessions is ludicrous. That child will never really understand this disease until he or she has seen or experienced it firsthand.

My mother, despite her addiction to prescription drugs, did her best to educate me about alcoholism. She spent much effort telling me, "If you drink, you are going to be a drunk just like your father and all of his family." Needless to say, this was not very effective. I was determined that I would never be an alcoholic and decided to smoke pot instead. I'm embarrassed to admit that, but this was my plan, which did not turn out very well.

I have long enjoyed doing presentations for family members. I like the group interaction and I often ask questions. One is, "Do you trust your loved one (the patient)?" To this day, I am still shocked by the number of people who raise their hand in the affirmative. I am very polite about asking someone to share why. I do not judge their reasoning, but I inform the group that trust is earned. No one simply deserves it. Trust will come back once someone proves his or her trustworthiness.

The next question I ask, "Is anyone in this room angry with their loved one?" Very few hands will go up. When their loved one seeks help, it is very common for the family's anger to go underground. Everything is rosy for a while, and then the anger starts to seep out. It can come out as sarcasm or overt rage. If suppressed long enough, it will take the form of anxiety or depression. I was told a long time ago by a truly wonderful therapist that anger is a smoke screen. He said that if our lives are threatened or endangered, anger is a survival mechanism that originates in the fight-or-flight center of the brain. Otherwise, anger is usually the response we

75

have when we are hurt. Anger is easier to deal with because very few of us can communicate the truth about what is going on.

Here is a personal example. When I went into treatment, my wife, Hannah, attended the family program as recommended. The staff members strongly encouraged her to attend Al-Anon meetings afterward, and she did attend two or three. As time went by, it seemed to me that Hannah was having a problem with anger. Our kids often commented about this, but I'd learned that it was not a good idea to talk to someone who is angry about their anger. For a long time, I felt that I deserved this. I thought things would get better. They didn't. I called my counselor in Atlanta and told him that my wife had become the biggest gripe that I had ever known. Jim laughed for quite some time and reminded me that he had warned about this. I still do not remember that warning! "Hannah isn't going to Al-Anon, is she?" he asked. I said no, explaining that she had gone briefly and then quit. Jim often cuts to the chase. "You know there is no way for you to get her there so you'd better start praying that she gets there on her own because your marriage will suck until that happens," he said. Something did happen, and I thank God because in just a few days of attending Al-Anon meetings, a different person came home one afternoon. Hannah's brother died from an overdose and the pain caused by this disease led her back to the doors of Al-Anon.

My addiction also affected our children in many ways. They were afraid of me because my behavior changed so quickly. They couldn't depend on me, and while I regret that, what I most regret was what I didn't do. I was not there for them, and they constantly feared their parents were going to get a divorce because of all the arguments and threats. I didn't think my children had been that badly affected by my addiction because they were so young. Jim told me that I was dead wrong about this but reminded me that children forgive. I realized the best gift I could give them was to be clean and sober and be there for them. I hope I have done that. If you are a family member or an alcoholic or addict who might be reading this, you need to know that your disease does have a major effect on your children. This is painful to consider, and your denial protects you from seeing this until you get sober. The payoff for everyone is much better than expected. Jim was right; children do forgive.

I could go on with this but I think I have made the point. Family members, you deserve to be happy and you can be happy even if your loved one chooses not to get sober. Some never will and that is sad, but please remember that you did not cause your loved one's disease. You cannot cure the person and you cannot make him or her get sober. Nor can you cause your loved one to relapse even though he or she may want to blame you for it.

Family members, just like patients, underestimate the power of this disease. There are many Al-Anon meetings available, including Al-Anon meetings for parents who have children with alcohol or drug problems. The people who can teach you the most are the ones who have been down that road. You can learn from their successes and from their mistakes. Although you may not be able to see it now, there is hope. There is no quick fix, and it doesn't take hours and hours of work to gain relief, but it does take effort. Do not depend on your loved one to get sober because he or she may not. Even if the person stops using, it will take a long time for the behavior to change. Some alcoholics or drug addicts stop using, but if nothing else changes, it is merely abstinence. Please don't confuse abstinence with sobriety. We will address sobriety in another chapter. Likewise, as Hannah can attest, abstinence by family members is miserable. There is a beautiful saying that is so true: "If nothing changes then nothing changes."

By far the biggest mistake that family members make is to enable the addicted person. Enabling means that you do something for someone that the person is perfectly capable of doing. One example is paying the rent when that individual is not making any effort to do it himself or herself. Also giving someone money repeatedly while that person makes no effort (but gives great excuses) to make his or her own income. Enabling allows the addicted person to continue to use and prevents them from experiencing consequences. I once told a mother that she was contributing to her son's death because of her outlandish enabling. He had no job and no transportation, so mom paid his rent on a very luxurious apartment and went grocery shopping for him weekly. She transported him wherever he needed to go, and he often verbally abused her. He sat in his apartment smoking pot, drinking alcohol, and watching television all day. Sadly, this young man eventually died.

It is extremely important to understand this idea of enabling. There are a number of reasons why this occurs, but the most difficult situation is when the addict is your son or daughter. This will be covered more in a separate chapter. In other relationships, enabling may occur because of fear. An example of this would be when spouses call their partner's workplace and makes some excuse why their spouse cannot come to work. The excuse, of course, is not the truth, although sometimes rationalization may allow them to believe what they are saying. The fear may come from the possibility that the spouse could be fired. It could also be an emotional or even physical fear of the repercussions that may occur if they do not do this.

Another level of enabling occurs because of codependency. This is often the hardest to understand because it is so pervasive. Codependency, briefly, is when someone bases their happiness on something or someone else. In this type of enabling, the spouse will go to any length to make their addicted partner happy. The spouses see it as their job to do so and many are masters at it, but surprisingly, they cannot see it. The defense mechanisms are incredibly powerful in these individuals. I have had cases in which an alcoholic or drug addict has reached the point of being done and cannot go on using. The spouse will sit next to them on the couch, pat an arm, and make excuses why this happened (it's his mother's fault or someone else's fault). Or, the spouse attributes the addiction to a mental illness and sometimes flat-out refuses to believe the loved one has a chemical dependency.

This is one reason why family members need to attend Al-Anon meetings. The enabling is often subconscious, and it often is easier to see it in others. Every situation is different, and there are no absolute rules. Al-Anon sponsors are especially helpful because they can give recommendations based on knowing the bigger picture. Enabling not only prolongs the suffering of the alcoholic or drug addict, it can even contribute to their death!

When the addicted spouse has been to treatment and is working on his or her sobriety, most couples will need marital counseling. During the "pink cloud period," when the crisis is over and life seems better, the reality is temporary. Again, the best example I can give involves the relationship between Hannah and me. As I was finishing up treatment, the staff "strongly" recommended that we get into marital counseling when I got back to Austin. Because Hannah was a registered nurse and I was a physician, we somehow came to the conclusion that we knew what to do by ourselves. We had no money; no one would hire me, and marital counseling costs money. The pink cloud dissipated and as I was approaching my first year of sobriety, we were on the verge of divorce. It was a horrible situation. I was still as crazy as a loon, and as I mentioned earlier, Hannah had a little anger problem. In a flash of sanity, we decided that marital counseling would be a good idea. On August 19, 2016, we celebrated thirty-eight years of marriage!

Often the entire family needs therapy. Young kids often are confused about what has happened. If they don't have some type of emotional outlet, this will come out as a behavioral problem, depression, or anxiety. The couple's parents certainly would benefit from education and therapy because they often are active in addicted person's life. It is to be hoped that the parents would be a part of the couple's support system. Achieving healthy relationships without professional help is like trying to pull an armadillo out of its hole by the tail. For those who don't know, doing that is next to impossible. The denial that exists in the in-laws and other family members is incredible. The lack of family support cannot cause the addicted person to relapse, but it can worsen the prognosis. For those seeking therapy, it is absolutely critical to find someone who is licensed as an alcoholism, drug addiction, or chemical dependency therapist. Unfortunately, many good therapists do not fully understand addiction and many do not believe it is a disease.

The family in recovery is a beautiful thing to see. It is not easy to get there. I will not kid you about this. It requires awareness that this disease affects everyone and that hope exists for those who put forth the effort. Several years ago, I had reached a point of burnout and I was questioning why I did this work daily. I seem to always hear about the tragic cases and I wondered if I was wasting my time. On that particular day, a young man came by my office and asked the secretary if he could speak to me. This young man was about thirty years old, and to tell you the truth, I did not recognize him. He walked in with what appeared to be his wife and young child. He told me that I had been his doctor seven years earlier and that he had remained clean and sober. He just wanted to thank me for helping him. He introduced me to his wife and two-year-old son. They seemed so happy, and that afternoon, I remembered why I was doing this work. I do not take credit for anyone's success. They have to do all the hard work. I consider myself the intermediary. Thank God, I also get to see many of these success stories. That is what keeps me going and makes the work rewarding.

I always have been very honest with family members by telling them that even though their loved one has completed treatment and seems to be doing well, there is no guarantee they will remain sober. Their hopes are up, and this statement sounds like a dream-killer. But failing to tell them would be like avoiding telling a family about a prognosis on their loved one's cancer or diabetes. The hope will come as they begin their own recovery as the loved one of a chemically dependent person. In doing that, they will improve the prognosis of the recovering individual. I am an eternal optimist when it comes to answering questions from families (and patients) about the prognosis. I tell them that there is a 100 percent chance of their loved one staying sober if they are willing to at least try. Anyone who has truly accepted this disease, is committed to working the 12 Steps of Alcoholics Anonymous, and incorporates the steps into their daily lives, is unlikely to die from this disease. If they have fully accepted that they will never be able to use alcohol or any other mood-altering drug on a casual or social basis, then I absolutely believe that that person will be successful. In the process, they will achieve the ultimate goal of sobriety that is described in the twelfth step of AA. I quote: "Having had a spiritual awakening as the result of these steps. ... This is the icing on the cake." Now if you happen to be an atheist or agnostic don't get your feathers all ruffled yet. I will talk more about this later!

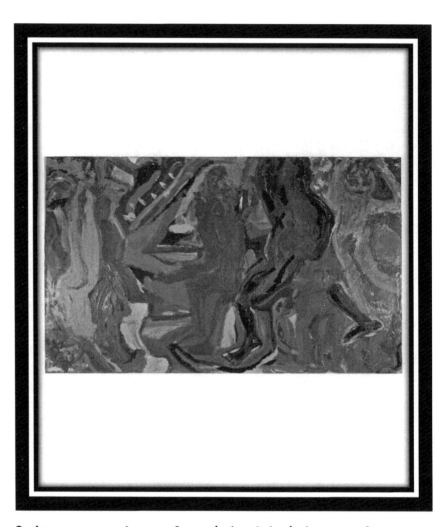

Guilt is a major driving force behind the behavior of enabling.

Chapter 8: For Parents of Chemically Dependent Children

First, the word "children" is not the most appropriate classification to use because most of these "children" are teenagers, young adults, and even older adults. But every parent knows: Our children are always our children despite their age. I have separated this topic into its own chapter because it is a growing problem that most parents do not understand this disease or know their actions (or inaction) may help determine its course. Parents endure an incredible amount of pain when their child is addicted. Many parents will say that when they had children, it was their first experience with unconditional love. This is a very powerful force to be reckoned with, so parents must understand that their love can lead to clouded judgments that can hurt, rather than help, their addicted child. Spousal addictions are not easy to deal with, either, but a spouse can reach a point where the pain is too much. They move on. This typically is not the case with our children, although it does happen. I am seeing more adult addicts who have not communicated with their family in decades.

As far as I know, there is no way to predict which, if any of our children, will have this disease. One day genetic testing may help with that, but this will likely be one of those lab tests that you wished you had not requested. Even knowing the results cannot predict the outcome because this is a multi-factorial disease.

I once heard Dr. Doug Talbott, founder of Talbott Recovery, say that it is likely every child born today who is genetically wired for this disease will manifest it because of the availability of mood-altering drugs and growing societal permissiveness toward drug use. By early 2017, eight states and the District of

Columbia allowed recreational marijuana use, and lawmakers in other states were filing bills to get the same consideration. At the same time, states were seeing record numbers of deaths from opioid prescription drug abuse. But we cannot blame society alone for our nation's chemical dependency epidemic.

I mentioned earlier that even children who may not be genetically wired or predisposed to addiction but use alcohol or drugs during their preteen and teenage years may progress as quickly as the genetically inclined individual. Dealing with alcohol and drug use in our young people is far more complex than with adults. We have addiction medicine professionals who specialize in that field. I could write much more on this topic, but my purpose in this chapter is to educate parents who are struggling.

In a perfect world, parents would be able to identify this disease in their children and seek appropriate help. As I've said, many parents do not believe alcoholism or drug addiction is a disease. Many parents will even argue that because they once smoked pot and used other drugs, this is just a phase their child is going through. That may be true. Around 90 percent of young people theoretically do not have this genetic predisposition. That would indicate nine out of ten may be just using and can stop on their own, or so we think. Remember, though, the incidence of this disease is higher in those who begin using at a young age.

What happens when the child has this disease and the progression begins? The lying starts to escalate, the behavior starts to deteriorate, and things that had been important in that young person's life are no longer. The parents are beginning to worry, often lying awake at night just waiting for their child to come home and thankful when they do that nothing bad has happened. Our denial has begun and it will grow as our child's disease grows. Enabling begins to take form as parents think this will somehow help their child see what they are doing. Guilt is a major driving force behind the behavior of enabling. Often parents feel guilty for not having spent more time with their child. By now, the family is walking on eggshells. Siblings become angry because all of the attention seems to be on the alcohol- or drug-dependent child. Siblings may also endure emotional or physical abuse from the alcoholic/addict, and the world is no longer safe to them. It's tough for parents to agree on how to respond, so the marriage fabric begins to fray. The alcoholic/addict has a great deal of power over the family members but this is mostly at the subconscious level. The parents find themselves making excuses for their child's behavior and often are speechless when someone asks how their child is doing. The parents may reach out to therapists or other professionals, but often, the confusion continues. By now, many parents believe their child's drug or alcohol use is their fault and, thus, the enabling continues.

I have often said that if high schools or colleges offered a course on how to set boundaries with other people, I somehow missed it. I suspect many others did, too. This is one of many reasons why the parents' Al-Anon group is critical. Parents must learn about setting reasonable boundaries because this is one of the few actions they can take that will benefit their child.

After years of practicing medicine in this field, I am convinced that adults and children with this disease must experience negative consequences before they become open to getting help. Consequences are subjective, and many parents struggle with the idea of allowing a child to experience pain or discomfort. Several years ago, a father called me to tell me his son had been arrested while his wife was in the background expressing her terror of what might happen to him in jail. The father had bailed their son out of jail other times. I suggested the parents wait a few days and go to as many parent Al-Anon meetings as they could during this time. Unquestionably, sitting in jail registers as a consequence. This act alone is not likely to alter their son's disease, but by stopping the other acts of enabling, the addict's using will begin to lose its charm. I cannot give a blanket recommendation to parents because each situation is different. One of the best examples is the teenager or young adult who is living at home, and the family is at the point of implosion. Most parents would say that if they kicked their son or daughter out of the house, they would have nowhere to go. They would be homeless, starving, and freezing to death.

Let me tell you something, parents: Most alcoholics and/or addicts are masters of manipulation. It is amazing to see their ingenuity and creativity. I have heard many parents say that when they asked their loved one to leave, their child threatened suicide. I, and I hope you, take suicide very seriously. Over the years I've had many teenage or young adult patients tell me they knew the threat of suicide would prevent their eviction. It worked every time. Thus, this threat was used to manipulate the parents and control the situation. I would never suggest that parents risk the possibility that their child may be suicidal. It is important to act on this statement and request an evaluation by mental health workers. First, and most importantly, you need to be sure your loved one is not suicidal. Secondly, dealing with the mental health authorities is not a pleasant experience, so if the threat of suicide was merely a threat to manipulate, it is not likely to be tried again.

The boundaries are parameters that you establish for yourself as the parent. They can be as simple as saying you will no longer allow your child to use alcohol or drugs in your home. Boundaries can be more complex, but the important thing is to be firm about the lines you draw. They can be changed later, if you choose. Just don't be an enabler. That is the worst possible action you can take for your child's well-being. As tough as it is, allow them to experience the consequences of their behavior. Try to work together with your spouse. It's critical that both of you be on the same page, because the alcoholic or drug addict will try to divide you to create more chaos. Do not make the decisions by yourself, and do not assume for a moment that your child's use is merely experimental. Above all, don't give them money! Not only is this enabling, it also creates a state of dependency rendering your child increasingly helpless. A common phrase in addiction medicine is "dependency breeds hostility." Think about that for a moment!

Parents often ask me if it is a good idea to drug-test their children. I tell them that if they choose to do this, they must have an action plan if the test is positive. This plan can be very simple or very complex. It must be something that is realistic and achievable. For example, if your child has one positive drug screen and you tell them they have to go to treatment, you are probably biting off more than you can chew. You should gradually increase the intensity of the consequences. I generally do not encourage parents to get into the drug-testing mode. It is much work and your child will give you every excuse in the world on why their test was not really positive. Our technology has provided access to hundreds of websites with details on how to beat a drug screen. It is a complicated process for many reasons. These websites teach a person how to use a drug that is not included on the drug screen itself. Standard drug screens test for the most commonly used substances. Many drugs are not included in the standard panel, including Suboxone, an opioid that is not detected on the usual drug screen because of its unique chemical structure. When a drug screen result is negative, the assumption that your child is not using may be incorrect. That is another reason I don't believe it is worth the effort to do the screens on your own. It is frustrating for all involved, and, unfortunately, a negative screen can't give you the assurance you're looking for.

Having a child who is an alcoholic or drug addict is one of the most difficult challenges I have ever experienced. All of the textbook knowledge in the world will in no way prepare you for what is to come. I never dreamed I would be visiting my child through a Plexiglas window at the jail. I recall a day when I was just relieved that my child was in prison because I knew where he was. My constant fear that he would someday have a fatal overdose subsided. I was ashamed that I could even think this, but no loss had ever caused more pain and grief in my life than this. I often wondered if people were looking at me with judgment, thinking I should have done a better job, especially given all I knew about addiction. At times, I, too, felt like a failure. Other times, I was sure the criminal justice system was not being fair with my son. I spent a great deal of energy being resentful towards police officers, lawyers, and judges. With the help of a group of parents who had been down this road, I found out that we all get put through the wringer of emotions that could make us look crazy even on a good day. I learned about detachment; you do not have to stop loving a person to practice this. I also had to look deeply at myself, at why I tried to take responsibility for someone else's behavior or why I based my happiness on how someone else was feeling.

My key message for parents is that you will need a support group to help you through these times. I can promise you there is no way to prepare yourself for what is to come when your child is an alcoholic or drug addict. This is a "learn-as-you-go" deal and there is no other way through it. Remember that there is always hope for your child. For your sake and theirs, never, ever give up. The young man I mentioned above is clean and sober today. He has returned to college and is making straight As. I know this is not a guarantee, but he has something now that is very precious to him. I believe when we reach that point, we have too much to lose. The decision to not use makes more sense than ever.

Finally, parents and other family members need to be prepared for the challenges of the aftercare period. This is the time just after someone has completed treatment. The family is out of the chaos mode and thrilled their loved one has finally "taken care of the problem." Family members are hopeful and usually supportive. The truth is, it cannot be assumed all is well because things can fall apart very easily during this period. Families, please know that it is fine to be hopeful, but do not set high expectations that your loved one will remain sober. Unfortunately, there is a strong probability that a relapse will happen soon.

I suggest that, if possible, you not allow your son or daughter to come back and live with you right after they have finished treatment. Of course, there are exceptions if your child is underage, disabled, or unable to afford sober house living. Fortunately, most large communities have one or more sober homes, dwellings rented to people in the early stages of sobriety. In Texas, there are no official requirements, so every sober home functions differently from another. The occupants may range in age from eighteen to seventy. They are always segregated by gender. There may be few rules or very strict codes of conduct. A house manager may live on the premises — or not. The owners or operators often are someone who is in recovery. The length of stay is variable, but six months to one year is a good starting point.

They can be a great solution, but I assure you that your son or daughter may not like the idea of living there. These used to be called "halfway houses," but that term conjures lodging with former prisoners who are being assimilated back into society. Regardless of the name, your son or daughter would much rather come back and live with you. That way, mom or dad can help take care of them, cook for them, and provide them with a comfortable cozy home.

The trouble with that is they miss a valuable learning opportunity. I can tell you from my personal experience that I learned more about sobriety in a sober home than I did when I was in treatment. Living with others in that environment requires you to function in the real world and learn how to interact with others. It is not easy nor should it be. When you have a houseful of newly recovering young people, one can only imagine the chaos that can happen. Yes, people do relapse in sober homes because they have a chronic, progressive disease. Sober homes do not offer the perfect world but they do provide a starting point for entry back into society.

Over the years, I have watched many parents allow their son or daughter to return home after treatment. My wife and I personally experienced this with one of our children. You would think a professional in addiction medicine would have seen this coming or that I would have learned from all the horror stories I had listened to from other parents. This was my child! This is a perfect example of why every parent should go to Al-Anon, and if it's available, a Parent Al- Anon Group. I did eventually realize I needed that support and went to the meetings.

Every person in early sobriety is hard to live with, even on a good day. For months, they will experience mood swings because of prolonged withdrawal combined with the stress of having to learn how to live in the real world without chemicals. As parents, you begin to wonder if your child has relapsed. Most parents desperately start trying to control the situation. You now lie awake at night and worry again whether to ask them to do a drug test. You wonder if you are just imagining what you are seeing, especially when they seem to be trying so hard! Remember all the things you used to worry about? Now there is more.

Parents, do not take on this burden alone. At Al-Anon meetings, you learn to stop the enabling. You learn about detachment and how to love your child regardless of the path they may take. Coming to grips with the fact that you have no power to alter the course of your child's life will be the most difficult thing you have ever done.

If you do allow your child to move back home after treatment, I recommend that you establish some rules — before they arrive. If you try to imagine what you would expect from a foreign exchange student who is living in your home and apply those same guidelines to your child, chances are better it will work out. Everyone shares the responsibility of making the house manageable for all living there. Communicating about who is responsible for what duties is key. Establishing a bedtime and setting the expectation that your child lets others in the home know if he or she is not going to be present is just common courtesy. At the same time, be flexible and accept that not everything will be done exactly the way you expect. That communicates that you are willing to do things in a different way. It is a sign of emotional maturity. The message to your child is: "I trust you to take care of yourself and your responsibilities." Using the example of hosting a foreign exchange student, would you allow them to sleep all day, stay out all night, not pay for any living expenses, or have a group of friends over at 12 a.m.? Apply the same expectations for your child. Above all, continue your participation in Al-Anon!

That is the nature of the disease. ... (E)veryone underestimates its power.

Chapter 9: Matching the Patient to Treatment

Almost everything I say in this chapter is refutable. But my opinions are based on thirty years as a physician working in addiction medicine and on my experiences as a recovering alcoholic and addict. To avoid the critics, I am going to keep this as simple as I can. Critics argue that the cost of treatment is not reflective of the quality of care. That may be true, but treatment is a broad range of actions varying from intensive, long-term, residential programs to a single visit with someone who has only just begun to shed some light on this disease.

The most difficult challenge I face is matching the patient to the type of treatment most appropriate for him or her. In my opinion, the provider absolutely must know as much as possible about a patient before talking about treatment options. One of the first things I say to a new patient is that every human being is different, and my goal is to learn as much as I can about their lives. I tell the person, "I am going to paint a picture of you with words." I give them ample opportunity to share what they think is important for me to know. This takes a minimum of two hours and sometimes longer.

When they finish, I ask my patients if there is anything else they think is important for me to know. Only at this point do I talk about the wide range of treatment options available. I describe treatment as a scale of intensity that ranges from doing nothing to entering a residential treatment center. I will tell them what I think is best, but they ultimately have to choose. Either way, I let them know I will continue to be supportive and respectful of them.

Before they decide, I often ask them to use their imagination to assume they came to my office for a different reason — to discuss the results of their blood work. I then tell them that I am so sorry, but they have a cancer called leukemia. I let them know they have a smorgasbord of options, ranging from doing nothing (resulting in them likely not living a year) to traveling to Houston for treatment, at the M.D. Anderson Cancer Center. I explain that cancer center likely will require chemotherapy, which would improve their survival prognosis by as much as 85 percent.

When I ask which they would choose, the vast majority pick M.D. Anderson. I then tell them that in deciding on a chemical dependency treatment, they need to consider it as a chronic, progressive, fatal disease — just like leukemia. I don't know how successful this approach is because I am talking to people who are full of shame and remorse. They often are clueless that they have a disease. Though this sounds reasonable to me, I am often left feeling bewildered by their answers. That is the nature of the disease. As I said earlier, everyone underestimates its power. When I suggest a certain type of treatment, such as intensive outpatient care, I always give the patient a list of three or more facilities that are appropriate. I do not refer people directly to the program where I serve as the medical director. Get a clean slate, folks!

I also make sure to tell them what "treatment" really means. I have to give an abbreviated version — or at least my abbreviated version. I tell them that an outpatient program spends a great deal of time helping them and their families understand why alcohol and drug dependency is considered a disease. This is very important because if you don't get this piece across, the outcome is not going to be good. Most patients accept their disease on an intellectual level. It will be quite some time before they are able to internalize this and accept it on an emotional level. Describing the biochemistry and brain centers that play a role in this disease often helps reduce the shame and guilt. Also, being with others who are there for the same or similar reasons allows these individuals to work through their own denial.

A big part of the time in treatment deals with this question: "How are you going to live in our society and not drink or drug but be happy?" This is the part that is the hardest for most people. It requires them to change their lives, and, as we know, most humans resist change. Although the chemicals have not been working, they are using now just to not feel bad. The idea of living a drug- or alcohol-free lifestyle seems incomprehensible at first.

I then tell them that the inpatient programs, whether they are thirty or one hundred twenty days, make the same demand for sobriety but with more intensity. Many patients need such a cocoon to obtain a level of safety because they have not been able to stop using on their own. In treatment, they will not have liquor stores and drug dealers readily available. Of course, inpatient care provides direct medical services for those who may have problems with withdrawal or other health conditions. I let them know that as inpatients, they won't be bothered by their work and even their family members. This all sounds good, but the first response is usually, "I can't bear to be away from my family. And I'm afraid I'll lose my job."

I respect those concerns because I faced them myself in 1985. A very wise man by the name of Jim Weigel pointed out that my family would be happy for me to away because I had been such an asshole. Jim did not hand out advice politely. He also said it was likely that "everyone at work knows that you are a drunk and a junkie. You were probably about to lose your job anyway. Your only hope of keeping it is to get sober." Jim was a master at knowing what he could get by with and what each individual was capable of hearing. I could clearly understand what he was saying, although someone else might have been offended!

When making treatment decisions, it is crucial to consider the type of drug(s) a person is using. Earlier I mentioned that benzodiazepines, the opioids, as well as marijuana, have a long withdrawal period. Therefore, a thirty-day program is insufficient.

As an example, a twenty-six year old woman came to my office and said she had been using 240 milligrams of OxyContin and six to eight milligrams of Xanax daily for four or five years. It is an absolute miracle that she had not died of an overdose from this combination of chemicals. She had overdosed many times but was fortunate to be at a hospital or with "friends" when this happened. The actual detoxification from these two drugs is tricky and it can take two weeks or longer. After detoxing, the brain will be able to put a few thoughts together, and the person will be able to participate in a group therapy session. I advised my patient that what some people call post-acute withdrawal will occur for several months and can last as long as a year. After I explained that, she told me that she wanted to attend an outpatient program because she was in college and had a job. She said she did not want to be away from either of them. She did not comprehend the correlation between drug dependence and the leukemia example I mentioned earlier. Her family supported her choice because if she dropped out of college and lost her job, everyone would know that she had a drug problem. Sadly, outpatient treatment did not work. Her family found her dead in her apartment three months later from an overdose.

If we were to use another disease such as diabetes as an example, it is easier to see the conflict. A person newly diagnosed with diabetes, once told that the disease can be controlled with changes in their diet and exercise, along with their strict adherence to medications, is more likely to accept those recommendations, rather than creating a self-prescribed alternative treatment plan.

For years we have known that relapse rates are extremely high in opioid addicts. While there are several factors involved, this one is critical: After a thirty-day program, the opioid or benzodiazepine addict has just started a prolonged withdrawal period. This phase does not have such acute symptoms as diarrhea, vomiting, and nausea. What the patient does have is a level of depression and/or anxiety, accompanied with insomnia, fatigue, inability to concentrate, and so on.

96

These symptoms are often severe, even "off the charts." These patients know that they could eliminate these symptoms in a matter of minutes — by using drug(s) again.

For treatment to be successful, consider whether the person has a support system. A person who has no real family support and lives in a drug-infested neighborhood is unlikely to succeed in outpatient treatment. A patient who does not have a job is also at risk in receiving outpatient therapy because one of the greatest triggers for relapse is idle time. Obviously, the patient could fill the days with 12-step meetings and visits to a therapist, but most do not.

Another challenge is the single mother who has three children for whom she is the sole provider. She has to worry about who will take care of her children if she moves to inpatient treatment and whether she will have her job when she gets out. I could go on giving examples, but my point is that matching the person to the most appropriate treatment is an arduous and very individualized process. As you may know, Americans have access to many good treatment centers. They vary in approaches, with some specializing in direct confrontation and others much less so. I am not sure which is best overall, but as a physician, I have to consider these factors depending on what I have learned about the patient.

For example, I might see an elderly Christian woman who is an alcoholic. Because of her upbringing and deeply entrenched beliefs, she probably would not do well in a program that is highly confrontational nor in one that allows messages laced with profanity. While this may seem minor to some, the truth is, this could make or break this woman's hopes of getting sober.

Some programs serve a large number of individuals who are involved with the criminal justice system. This alone does not determine whether the program is good. I tell patients that everyone is there for the same reason; it just so happens that those with legal concerns are the ones who got caught. Pride and ego may also affect someone's openness to what the program has to offer.

Since the 1930s, when AA came along, millions of alcoholics and drug addicts have become clean and sober, enabling them to live long, productive lives. NA, or Narcotics Anonymous, came along later because alcoholics did not want drug addicts in their meetings. Fortunately, that perspective is less common than it once was.

Although I took pains in my career to ponder the best way to address my patients' addictions, my experience has generally been that very few people agree to pursue what I recommend. I had to finally accept this and understand that the most important thing is that they start somewhere. We do know that the longer a patient is involved in structured treatment, the better the prognosis. I absolutely can say that those patients who experience a long-term, residential program have a much better chance for sobriety. Undoubtedly, many insurance companies and other professionals will disagree with this, arguing that the time and cost are too much. But when you see a patient who has been through ten outpatient programs and eight thirty-day treatment programs, it is obvious that the cumulative cost of failed short-term treatment is much greater than a long-term, residential program. And what about those who died as a result of inadequate attempts to address their addiction?

It may be obvious that I am not a fan of the managed care system for treating addiction. One experience in particular stands out from the latter part of the 1980s, when managed care was just developing. One day, I was told that I had to discuss a patient's case with another doctor who represented the managed care company. He was on the East Coast. I explained to him that I had a forty-five-year-old patient who had been shooting fairly large doses of heroin for the past eight years. After I finished describing the patient's needs, he advised me that he would "OK" for the patient to receive inpatient treatment for three days, but after that, he would have to be transferred to an outpatient program. I cannot tell you all that went through my head and came out of my mouth. I did inform the physician that he had sold out to medicine and that he was working as a prostitute for this company. I used some other colorful language that I'm not proud of but I meant every word of it. He informed me that he was going to report me to the medical board for abusive language, and I advised him that I was going to report him for practicing medicine in the state of Texas without a license. He did report me. After meeting with the director of the board's investigation program and explaining my story, he told me that he could understand why I was upset but that it was not OK for me to call another physician names. Point well taken, but it still did not address the failure to address a patient's rights to adequate treatment.

Lastly, the patient's motivation is critically important but incredibly difficult to discern. We do not have an instrument that will tell us how motivated someone is. After thirty years of experience in this field, I still have a difficult time assessing this. Some patients will give you a convincing story that leads you to believe they have surrendered and will likely be successful, only to have the family tell you later their loved one came only because it was treatment or prison time for a fourth DWI or a spouse's ultimatum. Of course, the patients themselves never mentioned this, which highlights the next point: There is a huge difference between commitment and compliance.

Sometimes you see the patient who is angry and hostile and very clearly tells you that he or she showed up only because someone else — usually their parents or spouse — forced them to come. These are difficult cases, and over the years, I have changed my approach several times. Now, I tell these patients privately that if they have no plans to get sober, they should not waste their parents' or family members' money on an expensive program, some of which cost up to $200,000. I also say the same thing to the family. I suggest that parents start saving up their money or find a good health insurance plan for their son or daughter because this is just the beginning of a very expensive ordeal. I point out that it is imperative to start somewhere but that they must look realistically at their options.

I assure you that the cost of a program does not correlate with its so-called "success" rate. It is true that even the most defiant patients have had some type of experience in treatment that totally changed their attitude. There are many of these cases. Families sometimes tell me that a certain program did not work for their family member. I tell them that no treatment center "works." The outcome is based on whether the patient is willing to do the work to stay clean and sober. Any program can provide the information and the tools for the path but no program can force the patient to use what he or she is given. If a program has not seemed to work, the likelihood is that your loved one was not ready or able to do the work. Blaming the treatment center only enables the addict to make excuses and continue progressing in their disease.

The environmental cues will trigger a cascade of neurological events that are far more powerful than the person's intellect or willpower.

Chapter 10: The Power of the Environment

I saved this chapter for now because once a patient finishes a treatment program or starts another method of recovery, everyone underestimates the power of that person's environment. You may have heard of an experiment performed by Russian scientist Ivan Pavlov years ago. He must have had a great deal of time on his hands or else he was very curious. Regardless, he had this idea that if he were to feed his dog and ring a bell, he could see whether there was some sort of connection between the two. Lo and behold, Pavlov discovered that when he rang the bell, the dog would anticipate eating and begin to salivate. This simple experiment demonstrated what is now called the "conditioned response." This means that some external stimulus (sound in this case) could elicit a response in the brain that was predictable.

Today, we understand that the brain's amygdala plays a key role in this conditioned response. The amygdala is heavily involved with positive and negative reinforcement, which means that consequences, such as an electrical shock, are also "remembered" by this part of the brain. It is the same part of the brain involved in chemical dependency.

So when Pavlov rang his bell, he proved the power of external, or environmental, forces on the brain. The dog's salivating response is also incredibly important. Salivation is an involuntary reaction. If I were to tell you to salivate, you would not be able to do that voluntarily. The autonomic portion of our nervous system controls this neurological response at the subconscious level. It is not at first a conscious thought. The subconscious brain is incredibly powerful and has enabled humanity to exist for hundreds of thousands of years. Consider the first human who met a saber-toothed tiger. I assume it turned out really badly because the brain did not register that this was a fight-or-flight situation.

Most people who use alcohol or drugs for the first time do so for common reasons. There are no new ones. They use to feel better, to be a part of the crowd, to feel at ease in uncomfortable situations, or to not feel anything at all. The effect of these chemicals on the normal person's brain is usually, but not always, pleasurable. In the alcoholic or addict, we have a response that is far different from that of normal people. This response is due to the massive release of dopamine from the nucleus accumbens. The fascinating thing about the effect of these chemicals is that for the addict, the chemicals seem to fix something in the brain that had not been working. The effect is perceived as positive because the person becomes much more social, more intelligent, more easy-going, or more comfortable in his or her skin. Sometimes, the effect is simply that the individual gets relief from the negativity, worry, or fear in the mind. The effect is positive and powerful because the addict has discovered at least a temporary solution to his or her problem(s). Like Pavlov's dog, a positive conditioning has now registered in the subconscious part of the brain.

The alcoholic or drug addict then returns to the real world and soon meets an old drinking or drugging companion. By now, the amygdala is firing, and memories of the pleasurable thoughts of using override the conscious thoughts (logic, judgment). Through a quick series of neurological connections, it now seems perfectly reasonable to conclude that it will be OK to use again. Do not blame the friend; it was the euphoric recall that led to continued using.

A similar thing happens when addicts return to a setting where they used to drink or drug. To put a very important point very simply: If you want to stay sober, you must avoid old friends you once used with. Period. Again, it is not their fault; it simply puts in motion a neurological event that is incredibly powerful. I expressed previously that early recovery is lonely, and this is one of the reasons. Developing friendships through the 12-step program is the solution to this problem, but it takes time. Parents and spouses take note: If you see your loved one associating with old friends in early recovery, you can be assured that a relapse has either occurred or is coming. Frequenting old hangouts or driving in neighborhoods where the chemically dependent person once used are also dangerous. Passing the liquor store where your loved one bought alcohol is another trigger. The threats are numerous. The important thing to remember is that the environmental cues will trigger a cascade of neurological events that are far more powerful than the person's intellect or willpower.

Another area of extreme importance involves relationships. Research scientist Carl Erickson gave a beautiful description of this topic in The Science of Addiction. We have known for years about a tendency of patients who are in treatment to get emotionally (and sexually) involved with another patient. It is also common for patients who have completed treatment to quickly get involved in a new relationship. Dr. Erickson explained that having sex or falling in love produces an effect on the brain that is closest to a chemical high. They involve the massive release of dopamine from the brain's nucleus accumbens, home of the pleasure center that I talked about previously. The part of the brain responsible for sex or propagation of the species is adjacent to the nucleus accumbens. In a roundabout way, the addict has found a "drug" through a new relationship that produces equal, if not more, euphoria than the drug or alcohol high.

Another well-known fact is the judgment of alcoholics and drug addicts remains impaired for quite some time after becoming sober. Let me explain. I have seen many bizarre situations in the treatment setting. One in particular made a strong impression on me. "Jack" had been married for twenty years and had two young children. His wife was very supportive, and he had a lucrative position in the family business. He was forty-five years old, and by his fourth week of treatment, he had started a relationship with a very attractive twenty-three-year-old woman who was a cocaine addict. He accomplished this despite the treatment staff's repeated efforts to handle the situation. He left our facility against medical advice with this young woman. I did not see or hear from either of them again, but the odds are high (no pun intended) that the outcome was not a positive one.

Most people can recall the first time they fell in love with someone. They remember a glorious, euphoric feeling that was unrelenting. We did all types of things to keep this relationship and maintain this feeling. Guess what? It is the same cycle that addicts experience with alcohol and drugs.

In my private practice, I see many people who have relapsed. I ask them a lot of questions because I have always been curious about the existence of common denominators. Yes, I ask about working the 12 Steps of AA and attending the meetings, but my third question is about relationships. I found many of them already were in a new relationship before treatment even started. Others are in relationships with a significant other who shares their disease. The probability of a person getting sober while returning to a relationship with an active alcoholic or drug addict is virtually 0 percent.

The important thing to remember is this: Getting into a relationship in treatment is a really bad idea. This is not a healthy environment in which to find a mate. Furthermore, getting into a romantic relationship in early recovery is an even worse idea. If the relationship ends up working out poorly, which is highly likely, the pain from this will be a huge trigger for using. Another issue is, a relationship takes a great deal of time and effort and can easily become a higher priority than getting involved in the recovery process. For patients who have a spouse or significant other with this disease, they face some very important, if not painful, decisions. If they decide to stay with that person, they have no chance of staying sober. Additionally, many patients are in relationships that subject them to emotional or physical abuse. It is unlikely the abuse will stop when the patient gets sober, so returning to that relationship is a set up to relapse.

Most of the time, patients tell me they began using again because of a failed relationship. To those who are in a long-term relationship that does not appear to be terribly unhealthy, addiction specialists suggest holding off on a decision to end that relationship for at least a year. This is not the time for life-altering decisions. That proved to be good advice for my wife and me when I became sober.

Chemical dependency takes a toll on the family but the good news is, healing is possible and will occur if everyone puts forth some effort. It is possible for this disease to stay in complete remission. The success rates exceed those of most other chronic, progressive diseases, even cancer, as long as the patient is willing to do one thing: Stop using mood-altering chemicals. If the person makes that one commitment, the potential for a good outcome is great.

Sobriety is a lasting journey with no destination.

Chapter 11: Sobriety

I almost hesitated to write this chapter because of the ongoing deep disagreement about how to achieve sobriety and define the term. I can only share with you what I have seen over these thirty years in the field. I am sure there are many ways to attain this thing we call sobriety. The word "recovery" might be more accurate because this is a never-ending journey, regardless of how you get there. Some people seek their religion or spiritual beliefs to replace alcohol and drugs. Some seek therapy, and others seek medication, along with professional help. Regardless, we must replace our disease with something else. I recall Dr. Talbot saying that when you give up alcohol and drugs, it leaves a hole in your soul. You can refill that hole with food, sex, material things, etc., or you can find yourself a God in whom to believe. For those of you who are atheist or agnostic, Dr. Talbot went on to say that you must think of "God" as something that you believe in and that brings passion to your life.

In the beginning, I mentioned that the grieving process begins to unfold as we give up something that has been important in our lives. Early sobriety is often very lonely because we have run off old friends with our using, and the newer ones (acquired while using drugs and/or alcohol) have to go if you hope to stay sober. One way to look at this, and I say it to every new patient, is picture yourself reaching a fork in the road. One road is predictable. Continuing down the road of alcohol or drug addiction has certain guarantees. You will end up in jail or some other institution. You often will not care whether you live, and death will eventually come because of your addiction. Of course, no one gets out of this world alive, but for addicted people, the misery and heartache before they bring on their own demise becomes unbearable.

The other road is sobriety and leads to a path that is unknown. That often is terrifying at first look, but at some point, we come to understand that there are no guarantees in this life. Most 12-step programs use the "chip system" indicating the number of months or years a person has not used alcohol or drugs. Somewhere along the way, someone decided that those who had many years of not using were the mystics and gurus whom we should look up to for counsel. I would argue that the amount of time someone has not used means little by itself. I am sure the chip system gives hope and many other things to the 12-step members. It serves as a tangible marker to track progress. It would be correct to say that someone truly did have "X" number of years of abstinence. This means that they did not drink or use drugs during that time, and that is all. Abstinence, by itself, is a miserable existence. Those of you who have tried to quit using for a time by yourself can understand this. It is so miserable that using again becomes more appealing.

Sobriety obviously includes abstinence but it also means being willing to change our behavior, our ideas, and, perhaps, even some of our beliefs. It is a clear movement away from our old lives, and in most cases, it requires us to attend to the spiritual portion of our humanness. Sobriety is also about taking care of our bodies and our emotional well-being. Many people believe that attending a 12-step meeting constitutes sobriety. Unfortunately, it does not; sobriety is far more than that.

Over the years, literally hundreds of people have told me that the 12 Steps of AA or NA are just not for them. It is true that some individuals have achieved sobriety without this type of program. I tell these patients that they are free to try some other method, but as far as I know, this approach is the most consistently proven method of staying clean and sober. I then ask if they are willing to take the risk. Herbert Spencer, the English philosopher who influenced Charles Darwin, wrote a beautiful paragraph that applies to patients who claim they have "another way:"

109

"There is a principle which is a bar to all information and proof against all argument and is guaranteed to keep a man or woman in everlasting ignorance...That principle is contempt prior to investigation!" That is why our treatment centers will direct someone to a path that has been traveled successfully by so many others.

It should be apparent that many people who want to get sober have no idea what the 12-step programs are about, and with ignorance comes fear. For that reason, I will do my best to help demystify what the 12 Steps of AA are about, so these fears may be lessened. When I was training the family medicine residents, I asked whether any had ever attended an AA meeting. Only one resident raised his hand. I then asked them to consider the likelihood of telling a person that they need to go to AA and the probability of that happening. There were many puzzled looks in this crowd. I told them that while they do not have to know the specifics, they must realize that there is a great deal of fear and anxiety in someone who has stopped using. The vast majority of AA members are wonderful people. They share so much humor and sadness in those meetings as well as opportunities to connect and learn with them. I told the residents they needed to understand that every meeting has its own unique personality. I advised them to tell their patients that they should attend several different meetings before developing an opinion about AA.

Several years ago, I was attending an AA meeting and things seemed to be going well. Suddenly, one of the participants began yelling rude comments and became increasingly agitated. The woman facilitating the meeting had no idea how to handle the situation. A psychologist friend was sitting next to me, and he decided he could help. Most professionals are taught to use some non-threatening statement to open up a line of communication. My friend said, "You seem very angry and upset." Bang! The gentleman slugged him, and things escalated from there. My friend learned that what he did is not a good way to approach someone who is high on methamphetamines and PCP. Imagine if this scene unfolded at someone's first

AA meeting. He or she might come away with a really bad idea about AA. Certainly, members at some meetings are still glamorizing their drug use, while some members at other meetings do little but complain about their problems. These are not representative of 12-step meetings in general. Most often, the members discuss solutions to their problems. There is a level of emotional honesty and a conveyance of hope that naturally draw people back to the meetings.

I also tell my patients that the purpose of going to meetings is the 12 Steps, which usually can be found hanging on the wall. Unfortunately, a person may show up who is insane, a pervert, an egomaniac, or whatever pathology you can imagine. They are there for less honorable reasons, such as meeting a potential dating partner. Thank goodness, the vast majority of people there are wonderful human beings. They will help you because, in doing so, they are able to stay sober themselves. I tell patients to not let any human being deter their pursuit of sobriety. Each meeting is different, and it's important to keep searching until you find one that fits you and helps you maintain sobriety. The same is true for those attending Al-Anon meetings.

One other dynamic that I suggested these residents know about is the significant role a sponsor plays in sobriety. Most people have no clue what a sponsor is or how to go about getting one. Sponsors are simply people who have completed the 12 Steps and are willing to help newcomers work the steps. That is their only job. Good sponsors will not try to be your therapist, nor will they tell you the things you would like to hear. Picking a sponsor is a highly subjective process. I suggest that a patient listen to the members talk for several weeks before asking someone to be their sponsor. Yes, it is just that easy. Find someone who has something that you want. It usually is a level of happiness and serenity you are not accustomed to having.

111

I have learned over the years that if individuals do not get a sponsor, they are unlikely to stay sober. The residents needed to understand the importance of sponsors and meetings, considering the number of people they would be seeing with addictions. Going to meetings is the beginning; obtaining a sponsor is the connection that begins and provides support throughout the journey.

The beauty of 12-step programs is they have no rules. Because most of us who are addicts have an inherent problem with authority and rules, it is a perfect fit. Here are some key guidelines for a successful relationship with a sponsor. First, males should get a male sponsor, and females should get a female sponsor. The reason for same-sex sponsorship does not need to be explained. It is only OK to have an opposite sex sponsor when a person is gay. Again, family members need to know that if their loved one does not get a sponsor, they should probably prepare for a relapse.

Going to meetings and obtaining a sponsor are actions that indicate the addicted person's willingness to change. Once this can be accomplished, the wheels are in motion. I once heard a psychologist speaking at an American Society of Addiction Medicine conference who said that the very act of getting out of the chair and going to a meeting will be more important for someone than what he or she might hear in a meeting. The action demonstrates willingness, and at least, the beginnings of commitment.

Sobriety is a lasting journey with no destination. I once heard AA speaker Sandy Beach, who died in 2014, say that if you pause for very long in this journey, you can settle for mediocrity. The possibilities for sticking it out, though, are infinite. I believe every human being is capable of making this transformation. Some are unwilling to give up their pride and pursue humility. Some refuse to give up the ego-driven mindset or their delusion of having power. Some are just complacent and have not accumulated enough pain yet. These are usually the ones who have

112

outstanding enablers. There are some who, for reasons I still don't understand, will never be willing to change and seem destined to die from their disease.

AA was founded in 1935, and I believe divine intervention was involved in developing the steps. Yes, a number of people contributed to this process, but it seems impossible that a group of alcoholics could come up with such a beautiful plan on their own, much less agree on it.

Janis Joplin once sang a song with this lyric: "Freedom's just another word for nothing left to lose." Sobriety is freedom from being a prisoner to alcohol or drugs. This freedom often comes at a high price.

Our brains are attempting to regain a biochemical balance that will take time to achieve.

Chapter 12: Simple Directions

I wrote this chapter because family members, alcoholics, and drug addicts who are just starting this journey often have a limited understanding of these steps. Treatment does present a general introduction to the 12 Steps, but those who have not had that opportunity may feel intimidated. Without going into depth, I will provide a brief summary of the steps because their meaning evolves within each individual over time. The steps are not hard but provide an essential guide to getting sober and staying that way. The spiritual principles are consistent with every major religion. Actually, they are not even inconsistent with atheism. I have often heard in meetings that one does not have to know who God is; the individual just has to know he or she is not God. The steps are worked with a sponsor, in numerical order, and I believe the overall directions are hard to beat.

Step 1: We admitted we were powerless over alcohol — that our lives had become unmanageable.

In my life, if I wanted something badly enough, I found that through work and effort there was nothing that I could not overcome — until I encountered this disease. Intellect and willpower could not keep me in remission. After four years of trying to stop on my own and failing, I became willing to give up on "my plan." True alcoholics or addicts cannot quit and stay "quit" by themselves. The day will come when we convince ourselves we can handle one drink or one pill. The delusion is remarkable in its power.

Years ago, one of my patients had a hard time understanding the first step. I have a great imagination and I like to explain concepts through stories. On that day, the story went like this: Imagine that every morning you walked out of your front door and there stood a man who was six feet eight inches tall. He had muscles that would make Charles Atlas marvel. Every day when the man walked out of the front door, the giant muscle man beat him up. This went on for several weeks, but

115

the man kept going out the front door and kept getting a beating. I asked my patient if he understood the problem and could he think of a way the man could have stopped the problem? My patient said, "Get a gun?" Some people, obviously, are more resistant than others. I suggested that perhaps the man could try another way out, the back door or even a window. To go out the front door was a guaranteed ass whipping (pain). He grinned and got the idea.

I am still in awe that accepting this notion of being powerless frees us from the struggle. My counselor told me that to truly be free, I had to include my lack of power in our government, the state of the world, my relationships, my desire to change other people, the criminal justice system, and virtually every aspect of my life. For quite some time I was not able to understand what Jim meant by that. Increasingly, though, I came to realize what he was saying was true. The basic idea is to honestly admit that what you have tried so far has not worked and that things are not going so well in your life. In fact, it has become unmanageable.

Step 2: "Came to believe that a Power greater than ourselves could restore us to sanity."

This step is often a major stumbling block for some people because of the "Power" and "believe" wording. Over many years in practice, I have had a number of opportunities to explain the second step. I find the best way to overcome the first part is to have patients admit that they are not God. Learning to trust takes time, but if they can give up the illusion of power over other people, places, and things, then they have a chance to learn to trust. Accepting the fact that we have become insane is also in this step. This was a problem for me as a physician. I did not believe that I had any symptoms of insanity, which I defined as having hallucinations and being out of touch with reality. The last part of step 1 says that we admitted our life had become unmanageable. In the process of taking an honest look at my behavior, it became clear that I was not acting normally. If you define insanity as repeating the same thing over and over and expecting different results then, yes, I had to admit that I was insane.

Step 3: "Made a decision to turn our will and our lives over to the care of God as we understood Him."

This is a very big one and most people dig in their heels on this step. I said earlier that by the time most of us reach "the bottom floor of this elevator," we are spiritually disconnected. I point out to my patients that this step requires us to make a decision, not a promise. That decision can change from day-to-day or hour-to-hour. Alcoholics can handle a temporary decision better than they can handle an absolute commitment.

The step goes on to state, "As we understood Him." The problem seems to be that most people focus on the word just before this, which is "God." Every person pursuing sobriety comes from a different place depending on how one's "belief computer" was programmed. Some, like me, were forced into the Southern Baptist religion. My mother dragged me to church every Sunday morning, Sunday night, and almost every Wednesday night for eighteen years. We also attended every revival within thirty miles of Marshall, Texas. I listened to preachers tell me that if I even thought about something sinful it was the same as acting on it. I would be going to hell. I was doomed, and I knew it. The way my mind works is, you might as well do it if you are going to hell anyway. Some patients were never exposed to religion or were raised as atheists or agnostics. Almost everyone who reaches this step runs into a problem. Based on who we are programmed to be, which belief is the "right" one? I have no idea. At this point, one needs to become open to other ideas. The "how" of sobriety involves honesty, open-mindedness, and willingness.

Step 4: "Made a searching and fearless moral inventory of ourselves."

Most people stop on step 4. Over the years I have seen hundreds of people relapse. Many will say that they tried the 12 Steps without elaborating. I would often ask if

117

they had attempted the steps, and if so, how far did they get? In my experience 100 percent will either tell you that they did not do step 4 at all, or admit that it was, at best, a half-assed effort. I suppose that many people struggle with the word "moral." This step does not say to focus only on the bad, although it is easy to forget that there is much good in every human being. Virtually all of us fear the idea of being absolutely honest with ourselves and then have to admit what we see to another human being. It is no wonder that many alcoholics and addicts stop at this point. That is why a sponsor is so terribly important. The sponsor can gradually guide someone into this step and explain the overall purpose. Over time, the addict will develop trust in the sponsor, opening the door to sharing the moral inventory.

This step is not about coming up with every negative detail from your life. It is about looking at the general patterns and seeing the areas that you can change. My sponsor once told me, "You are not that complicated, you keep doing the same thing over and over." I suppose the best way to explain this step involves something that I wrote about earlier. Some of us have an opportunity in our lives to stop and take a look at how we think and what we believe. Our brain has been programmed to provide this information, and we have a new chance to decide what parts of our thoughts and beliefs make sense and what parts are inaccurate and fail to serve us well. Only by becoming aware of this can we begin to make changes.

I mentioned previously the term "neuroplasticity." We are absolutely capable of changing our thinking and our beliefs if we are able to be aware of what is not accurate. This step is not a confessional. I want to re-emphasize the importance of looking at the positive parts of ourselves. Perhaps guilt and shame have prevented us from seeing that. A sponsor can help us balance the negative with the positive.

These first four steps tend to be the most difficult. Step 5 involves admitting the exact nature of our wrongs to ourselves, another human being, and God. I really

118

wish another word could have been used here instead of "wrong." Please don't get hung up on one word. I would say that the vast majority of addicts are masters at picking out inconsistencies. I was in my second week of treatment when I came up with a list of problems in the program. I had a group of counselors who I thought were incompetent, and I went so far as to say that the grammar used in the AA book indicated that the people who wrote it were not very bright. I looked for the flaws as I had done all of my life, and I can tell you today that it was a waste of time and energy.

Steps 6 and 7 involve acknowledging our inaccurate thinking and the behavior it causes. In step 6, we are admitting our way did not work and we begin to look at our shortcomings as something we no longer want. Once again, we are asked to rely on a Higher Power to remove our shortcomings.

In step 7, we "Humbly asked Him to remove our shortcomings." The key concept here is humility. I was always confused by this word, and my brain could only interpret it as meaning the same thing as "being humiliated." Again, I was wrong. I once asked a dear friend about this and he said that humility only comes with being honest with ourselves and other human beings. It is a process; it does not occur as an event.

Step 8: "Made a list of all persons we had harmed and became willing to make amends to them all."

Now for some of us, this seems like a lengthy process. One typical problem that comes up is we are making a decision about whether we have harmed someone. Often, we are way off base. Most of the people we believe we have harmed would not even remember our names. They usually have not spent even ten seconds thinking about how we have harmed them. Our ego at this point still is very powerful. We believe we are important and powerful enough to have had an impact on the person. I handed my sponsor a list for step 8 that was two legal

119

pages full of my transgressions. He handed it back to me and said, "You are not that important." This is an important step and it should be taken seriously. The task, at first, appears formidable, but, again, sponsors help us to keep it simple. Please note that the step says willing to make amends. Somehow most of us tend to miss this word. The fear of making amends often stops us in our tracks.

Step 9: "Made direct amends to such people wherever possible, except when to do so would injure them or others."

The phrase "except when to do so would injure them or others" can cause complications for the addict working this step. By now, hopefully, we are getting closer to realizing that our own thinking is not very accurate and that we must depend on others who have been down this road.

For most of us, our brain chemistry is still in turmoil. Our brains are slowly healing, but some of the circuits are continuing to misfire. Our brains are attempting to regain a biochemical balance that will take time to achieve. I still find it fascinating that our concept of reality is a function of our brain chemistry. This is incredibly powerful. Our reality is truly the reality we experience, just as the paranoid schizophrenic really does believe that the hallucinations and delusions are true.

In chemical dependency, the brain chemistry changes during the time the addict is using drugs or alcohol. This may encompass years of chemical use. When you add a chemical to the body, it causes the body to release a tremendous amount of dopamine from the nucleus accumbens. In the case of opioids, a profound deficiency of endorphins is the body's response to the drug. It makes sense that it will be some time before your thinking is accurate.

Step 10: "Continued to take personal inventory and when we were wrong promptly admitted it."

In sobriety, we are changing our actions and how we think and behave. Change involves repeatedly identifying the negative thoughts or actions and replacing them with something positive. Repeating this behavior allows our brain circuitry to use a different pathway. Our old way of thinking is now replaced with a healthier one.

The second part of step 10 involves taking action to change, rather than just thinking about it or even acknowledging what we want to change. Most of us do not like admitting we were wrong, but when we are, we have to face our wrongs with honesty. Because dishonesty was a glaring problem most of us uncovered in step 4 and because it is very dangerous for us in sobriety, we really have to do this step continuously to stay sober. My dear friend Charles was the person who helped me with this concept.

He would ask me if I had lied to anyone since the last time we had met. Of course, I had — but "not big ones," I would say. He then told me to go to each person and tell him or her that I had lied. I did not like the idea because I felt embarrassed and foolish. But I did what he said. He explained that the word "promptly" was in the step for a reason. He said I would eventually quit telling people lies because it made me feel embarrassed each time I had to go back and tell them I had been dishonest. "Promptly" could also mean stopping myself in a lie I was just about to tell. Being honest seemed so much easier. Step 10 is about being able to walk down the sidewalk and not feel like crossing the street when someone walking toward you is a reminder of a wrong you have not made right.

Steps 11 and 12 involve the development of the spiritual aspect of who we are, whatever that may be. The core of these steps, though, is the basis of the entire program, which is to serve others. As we help other human beings, we begin to move away from selfishness and self-centeredness. The AA book says that those two words are the root of all of our problems. The philosophy of giving to receive is the foundation, I believe, for every religion. Even those individuals who avoid

121

religion will in time learn that this idea is a law of nature; it is not merely confined to religion.

The 12 Steps of AA are tools to be used on a journey toward a spiritual life. The addicted person will never fully complete any of these steps. They are in order for a reason. It does not take a tremendous amount of work and effort to move through this 12-step plan. In most cases, the most important thing we can do is to quit certain behaviors. It is a very simple process that we tend to complicate. I truly wish I could explain or teach a person to give up the battle, for that is what it is. Neither I nor anyone else can make that choice for them. After years of trying to convince others to make that choice, I have finally come to believe that each person is on his or her own journey. The best I can do is offer hope by reinforcing that a solution to the problem is within reach. Yes, it is a remission rather than a cure. I tell patients the only thing they have to be sure of is understanding that alcohol and drugs will never, ever work again. If they can completely accept this, then the rest is very easy.

I have encouraged patients to look at (drug) screening as just a part of their support system.

Chapter 13: Random Drug Screening

I included this chapter for two reasons. The first is because I promised to do so earlier in the book. The second is that I have worked with impaired health professionals for thirty years, and random drug screening is used by almost every medical professional organization. The Department of Transportation started random drug testing long before it became popular in the private industry. The DOT does literally millions of drug screens per year and its policies are still the gold standard today. After several years of working with the Travis County Medical Society Physicians' Health and Rehabilitation Committee, I got my Medical Review Officer certificate to understand better how these screening programs work.

After thinking about this for years, I tell everyone who is subjected to drug screening the sole purpose is that it may someday be the only thing preventing a relapse. The looming possibility that they might be screened at any moment is a deterrent. This deterrent by itself will not work forever, but it can be an effective prevention tool. For it to work, a patient has to be motivated in some way to use drug screening as an insurance policy. People who remain intent on using will, and if they are intent on beating the screens, they may do so for a while. The nature of this disease is that it is chronic and progressive. Eventually, the disease always wins.

Another benefit of drug screening is that it provides the addicted person with an objective means to show others that he or she is not using alcohol or drugs. That is important because most people don't trust addicts to begin with. People with addictions — myself included — have lied to our loved ones and employers often, professing, "I am not high. OK?"

At the same time, society must be cautious in relying on drug screening or risk doing great damage, not just to recovering alcoholics and addicts, but to people in

124

the workforce. While very good, the technology is not perfect because human beings are involved in the process. Also, our society has provided us with an incomprehensible number of drugs that can interact and cause what we once called a "false positive" result. Now that is an interesting way to look at this. There is nothing false; the test result is negative. This is why I became certified as a medical review officer. The course for this certification was one of the best I have ever taken. I learned that the details of interpreting drug screen results are very complicated. No need to elaborate here, but when your job or your medical license is on the line, you want to be sure all the cards are on the table. Let me explain.

Twelve years ago, a test that could detect the slightest amount of alcohol in the body, ethyl glucuronide, became available in the U.S. The test was so sensitive it could detect alcohol intake for up to eighty hours after it was ingested. Ethyl glucuronide is a minor product that is made when the body metabolizes alcohol. Minor means that only a small quantity of EtG (ethyl glucuronide) is produced, while the majority ends up as carbon dioxide, water, and acetic acid. Just one problem: Alcohol is readily absorbed through the skin and is present in a vast number of medications, shaving lotions, and aerosols. The term "environmental alcohol" was used to describe an unintentional taking in of alcohol. So a fairly large number of people were having positive EtG tests, but there really was no way to distinguish between environmental absorption and intentional ingestion. Even the medical review officers weren't sure how to handle this. Someone decided that very low levels of EtG represented absorption through the skin. Sounds good, but it's not true. Those who had quantities of one thousand nanograms per milliliter or higher were assumed to have ingested alcohol. Unfortunately, this is not completely accurate.

This great test had now become complicated, but that didn't stop people in the medical and legal professions from interpreting such results as proof the individual had used alcohol. With that said, I was asked to testify in a trial for a physician

125

who had lost his medical license because he submitted a urine specimen that tested positive for EtG around three hundred fifty nanograms per milliliter. The physician's case was before the Texas Medical Board, which I truly admire and respect. Board members have a tremendous challenge and do a fine job with a few exceptions, and this case just happened to be one of those. The physician's attorney called me and said that his client was married with two kids and had not worked in almost a year because the board had taken away his medical license. Of course, the attorney's last statement was that the physician had no money. So I volunteered to testify, a chore I absolutely hate. I once had a friend tell me that he would rather have a barbed wire enema than testify in court. I don't know that I would go that far, but close.

The medical board had an expert who testified that it was possible the doctor had ingested alcohol. The expert claimed that if the physician had consumed alcohol sixty to seventy hours before being tested, the EtG level would simply be decreasing over time and the test would not have detected what could have been a higher level. The hearing was brutal, but I learned a long time ago that all you have to do is be honest and not let the other attorney rattle your cage. To be brief, the district court ordered the medical board to return the physician's license.

I used this example not to focus on physicians or medical boards but to underscore the importance of accurate interpretation of drug screen results. Many other scenarios can lead to such false positives. I hate that term. By now we know that several antidepressants will show a false positive for benzodiazepines. Ibuprofen has caused false testing results for amphetamines, and several anti-fungal agents can produce a positive test result for sedatives.

Another example, which most people may be aware of, is a positive test for morphine from eating poppy seeds.

Poppy $\rightarrow$ Heroin $\rightarrow$ Morphine

Indeed, a small quantity of morphine can be found in poppy seeds. A person would have to eat a truckload to get high, but we used to believe that it took large quantities of poppy seeds to generate false test results. Again, we were wrong. Now we know that consumption of one bagel covered with poppy seeds can cause a positive test result. Thank goodness we can now determine whether the person ingested or injected morphine, rather than nibbled on poppy seeds. As you would guess, the outcome of the test results would have a major effect on the person submitting the sample.

Today, computerized random drug screening programs are available to the public. The purpose of these is twofold: As I have mentioned, they provide a deterrent to relapse and a proof of sobriety. The participant calls a toll-free number every day and a computer randomly decides who will be tested that day. It is very complicated to explain but easy to administer. Of course, few people want to agree to this type of program. I have encouraged patients to look at screening as just a part of their support system. Because the disease is multifactorial, the treatment must be as well.

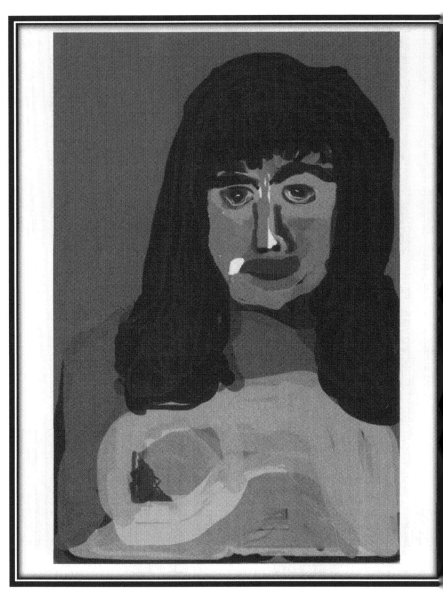

I can still see her smiling.

Chapter 14: Adult Children of Alcoholics

Many books have been written on this topic, so I encourage those who want more detail to read one of them. I mentioned very early in this book that a family history of alcohol or drug addiction increases the likelihood of having this disease. When someone grows up in a family in which one or both parents were chemically dependent, the stakes get higher. For years, treatment program experts have known that growing up in an alcoholic family affects the patient, but they placed little emphasis on this dynamic. When I entered treatment in 1985, I was asked to describe my family. I informed the therapist that I had grown up in a very normal family and that it was none of her damn business.

I can still see her smiling. I am sure she must have thought I was an idiot. It did not take long for me to realize that what I called normal was just my perception. I really didn't think my family was any different from your typical East Texas family. That's where I was wrong. My family was colorful and a lot of fun. I was not aware of any violent tendencies, although I noticed that most of my family members would disappear for days at a time for reasons unknown to me. We occasionally had a few surprises, like the sudden appearance of my unknown Uncle Ross, whom I mentioned earlier. Then we had our share of what everyone called episodes of "being under the weather." I clearly recall a family reunion when my grandmother was found sitting on the ground leaning against a picnic table. I really thought she was dead because she really looked bad. But I was only twelve or thirteen, so what did I know? My mom told me that my grandmother was having one of her dizzy spells. Well, grandma was drunk and I am still to this day amazed how the family could keep on with the reunion and not really stop and deal with her.

Years later, my grandmother would call me from the nursing home and ask me to help her run some errands. I had just gotten my driver's license, and she was willing to pay me $5 to escort her around. As we were driving down the highway, she abruptly told me, "Turn left right here," which I did, only to find myself about to enter the drive-through of the Bull of the Woods Liquor Store. My grandmother seemed to know the guy at the window and assured me I wasn't doing anything wrong. She ordered five half pints of Old Crow and I noticed the attendant had an odd look on his face. I turned to look at my grandmother and saw she had her dress hiked up and already had three of the five half pints stuck in her hose. They were supported by what I was to later find out was called a "garter strap." Lacking a hole to crawl into, I decided the best way to handle this was to not say anything at all. The nursing home often called my mother to report that my grandmother appeared drunk. The caller just could not understand how this kept happening. I made many $5 bills and never opened my mouth. Later, I found out that my sister was doing the same thing.

I learned a lot growing up in my family, but there was a dark side that was difficult to understand. The book, Adult Children of Alcoholics, helped me understand most of this. The author says that the children in the alcoholic family learn three important things: They learn to not talk, trust, or feel. I had learned those lessons well. I would add that you do not come out of an alcoholic family with much self-esteem.

I did have wonderful parents. They gave me a value system, a work ethic, and even integrity that I treasure today. They did the best they could. I didn't know for a long time that they, too, had grown up with parents who were both alcoholics. So when the family therapist told me that alcohol and drugs were affecting me long before I ever used them, I finally understood.

A substantial number of people have coexisting mental illness and chemical dependency

Chapter 15: Barriers to Success

The road to sobriety can be long and twisting, but there is always hope for those who are willing to do the work that's required to stop using. Some of us will run into roadblocks on the path to success. These barriers need to be understood and overcome. Among the obstacles are:

1) Entitlement. In my experience, a sense of entitlement is the most difficult obstacle to overcome. Most people assume that entitlement is typical of rich or famous people, but this is far from true. Entitlement occurs whenever people believe they deserve certain privileges because of their position or perceived position in society. Our materialistic culture has contributed to an epidemic of people who somehow feel they deserve something. The days are fading when parents taught their children to earn an allowance or instructed them on having a good work ethic. Many parents in good faith want their child to have the "things" they didn't have when they were growing up. Meanwhile, a parent may hold two jobs — or both work long hours — missing out on time to guide and enjoy their children. Sadly, many parents substitute material possessions for love, affection, and nurturing. I see so many young people who say that they really never knew their parents and that their parents expressed love by buying them what they wanted. While we see many wonderful, caring families, we also have a population of individuals in all age groups who exhibit entitlement behavior. It may indicate poor self-esteem and perhaps feelings of inferiority. More often, it is used as a defense mechanism. These individuals are masters at identifying any weakness or inconsistency in any system and often justify leaving a group or a treatment program because of this. Many will violate the basic rules because they don't believe the rules apply to them. Those are the people who are often asked to leave a program, and they will go on to justify using again, citing that rejection.

While many of us will never have to worry about this, I have seen a lot of cases in which extreme wealth seemed to be the fatal factor. One I will never forget. I was in my first year of sobriety and I was working a night shift at a local minor emergency center. A young man of thirty-two years-old came in with some type of respiratory infection. I couldn't help noticing extensive track (needle) marks on his arms. I asked whether he thought he might have a drug problem, and he acknowledged being an IV heroin addict but didn't consider it a problem. I had learned to not be confrontational or judgmental so I moved the conversation along. He was a very pleasant man, and we were joking back and forth as he left. I saw him two or three more times in the emergency department and the last time was because of abscesses on his arms from the intravenous drug use. I told him that if he ever wanted help to stop using, he could call me. He took my card, smiled, and asked me if I knew who he was. I honestly didn't, and then he continued to tell me that he was worth millions of dollars and that he had more money in his checking account than I would ever make in my life. He then told me that his parents had been very wealthy but that both had died a few years earlier from alcoholism. He had been using before he came in, so his moods were up and down. He left, and, again, we had been joking. The visit went well, and I liked this young man. I really didn't know much about him, but I could tell he had endured much emotional pain in his life. He did not return for his follow-up visit, and four or five days later, I saw his obituary in the newspaper. He had been found in a hotel room with a needle still in his arm. He had died from a heroin overdose. I remember my last words to him as he was leaving. I said that all of this money might someday kill him. I remember him laughing and saying that it probably would. And it did. No, the wealth itself did not do this. He had been arrested numerous times, but he could afford the best lawyers, preventing him from experiencing any significant consequences. Of course, he never faced financial difficulties, nor was his job ever threatened. He never had to work. I am absolutely sure many folks with great wealth are wonderful people, and their financial position is not a barrier. That is because wealth does not make any person entitled. Entitlement is a state of mind.

2) Codependency. The truth is, I really hate this word and hesitated to even use it. Back in the 1980s and 1990s, this word seemed to be applied to almost everyone. Treatment centers sprang up to treat the vast number of "codependent" people.

Codependency means that a person bases his or her happiness on something that is external to them. This is not Webster's definition; it is Dr. Munden's. I do not mean to make a joke of this word because it is important to understand why it is a barrier to successful sobriety. The most common "object" of codependency is, of course, another human being. The best way to help you see this is with an example. Remember, all of these are actual cases.

Mary (not her real name) was twenty-seven when she came to treatment from a hospital where she had been admitted for a heroin overdose. From the first day of treatment, Mary could do little other than talk about her boyfriend. While there was no proof, her parents reported that the boyfriend was frequently physically abusive. Despite looking at her multiple arrests, overdoses, and treatment for abscesses on her arms, she said she could not stay in treatment because she had to be with her boyfriend. She left after one week and died six months later from a heroin overdose. I could give hundreds of examples, but my point is, the codependent individual will jeopardize everything for the approval or love of another person. The relationship, however good or bad, is the highest priority. Unfortunately, if you base your happiness on another person, a lot can go wrong. They die, disappear, or simply leave. It is never a good idea to have all of your eggs in one basket.

3) Mental illness that is untreated! I have mentioned this in previous chapters, but it bears repeating. A substantial number of people have coexisting mental illness and chemical dependency. Individuals who have been exposed to sobriety or who

have attained extended time in recovery know at some level that alcohol and drug use will not give them much, if any, pleasure. The chemicals have stopped working. Oh, they may feel a fleeting moment of euphoria in the beginning, but it is not sustainable. So it is pain that is the usual driving force for a relapse. I mentioned this in an earlier chapter. Mental illness is painful, and no one volunteers to have it.

Over the years, I have seen a number of patients who had relapsed multiple times. They would tell me they went to a 12-step meeting, got sponsors, worked the steps, and did everything possible to stay sober. They would sometimes stay sober for a year or more. I started asking patients like this how they felt during those periods of sobriety. They would say, "It was OK, but my life was better than when I was drunk." They were not experiencing any joy. Many of these patients suffered from an undiagnosed depressive disorder and were incapable of experiencing the happiness that comes with recovery.

Of course, there is flip side. Many individuals seem to want to have a mental illness. Often, family members support this notion and use the term "self-medicate," implying their loved one relapses to treat some sort of discomfort. Guess what? This is why almost every person relapses. But some of those who relapse sit on their ass and are unwilling to look at their character defects or pursue a life of honesty and making amends to the ones they have harmed. I assure you, these people will be in pain. So, indeed, they do self-medicate!

4) Intelligence. Yes, this is correct. No textbook would say this, but I have seen college professors and other professionals who could never grasp the idea that intelligence alone would not get them sober. Yes, they had accomplished much with their intelligence, but it just wasn't enough to solve this problem.

5) Co-addictions. We are all somewhat familiar with eating disorders and gambling. The list of addictions has gotten much longer and includes pornography,

work, video games, and many others. From my experience, addiction to video games is almost an epidemic, especially in young adults and teenagers. Although it can exist by itself, it is very common to see video game addiction coexisting with chemical dependency. Years ago, workaholism was the most common co-addiction and was alluded to in the AA Big Book. That is certainly not the biggest problem today. If anything, we are seeing what I term "refusal to workaholism." What I mean are individuals who seem to have no work ethic or desire to be employed. Often, loved ones have enabled this attitude. Co-addictions frequently are overlooked in treatment because of the severity of the chemical dependency. Most patients don't bring up their other issues because, frankly, they do not see the co-addictions as a problem. But it is necessary to realize the existence and importance of co-addictions. Talk about this with the treatment staff, your doctor, or therapist. Co-addictions are very treatable. Many individuals carry much shame with these addictions, just as they did with their chemical dependency. Family members, if you suspect your loved one has a co-addiction, start talking about it. Don't judge or accuse; remember, no one can argue with your concern.

6) Contempt prior to investigation. You may not be familiar with this barrier, but it is a common one. As Herbert Spencer, the British philosopher, biologist, and sociologist, wrote during the Victorian era:

"There is a principle which is proof against all argument and a bar against all information that is guaranteed to keep a man or woman in everlasting ignorance."

That principle is contempt prior to investigation. This should speak for itself. Here is the perfect example. After I encouraged a patient to get to AA meetings, he informed me that those meetings were not for him. He was not like those people, he said. When I asked him if he had ever been to an AA meeting, he responded, "No!" His own biases had left him ignorant.

Physicians, nurses, pharmacists, and dentists are not stupid people, but they have not received adequate training to diagnose and treat the disease of chemical dependency.

Chapter 16: To The Doctor

As I was preparing to start this chapter, my wife asked me how many physicians had contacted me in the past thirty years to ask questions about addiction issues with their patients. I thought for a moment and my response shocked even me. "Four or five," I said. That leads me to believe very few physicians will read this book. Patients and family members, it will be up to you to pass this information along to the medical profession.

I have always advised patients that it is their responsibility to tell their primary care doctor and any other physicians they see that they are in recovery from the disease of chemical dependency. Of course, I follow this statement by telling my patients that their physicians probably won't have any idea what they are talking about. I suggest they have their doctor talk to an addiction medicine physician before prescribing any mood-altering medication. Furthermore, I ask my patients to talk with their pharmacist (and perhaps their sponsor) just to be sure. I also tell them if they are having an elective surgery, they should ask the surgeon to consult with an addictionologist, a physician who studies and treats people with chemical dependency.

During some of my lectures, I make an offer to everyone in the room: Anyone with questions about a medicine they are prescribed can call my office, free of charge, for a consultation. I have presented this lecture to twenty- or thirty thousand people over these past thirty years and I have received less than fifty phone calls taking me up on this offer. This leads me to believe patients and families may underestimate the dangers of prescription medicine. Perhaps I give crappy lectures, but I would like to believe the prior sentence is true. When you consider over half of the patients who relapse will do so on prescription medications, this becomes an important issue to talk about. There is no doubt we have the finest, most advanced medical profession in the world. I have no intention of criticizing our medical

138

professionals, but it is about time for us to address a problem most people don't want to talk about. Physicians, nurses, pharmacists, and dentists are not stupid people, but they have not received adequate training to diagnose and treat the disease of chemical dependency.

In 1992, I was putting a tin roof on a barn at our small "ranchito" in the country. I was hurriedly climbing a ladder and I ungraciously fell fourteen feet to the ground. A pile of rocks showed up precisely where I landed, breaking my collarbone and two ribs, chipping my shoulder blade, and partially collapsing a lung. Let me tell you, I am not a tough guy. I do not like pain. In the emergency room, a very bright, energetic female physician attended me. I told her up front I was a recovering drug addict and alcoholic. I also wrote those details on my check-in sheet under "other medical conditions." She smiled at me politely and then asked me if I wanted a shot of Demerol because my collarbone was clearly broken. I informed her I would absolutely love a shot of Demerol, but because I was a recovering opioid addict, I did not think it would be a good idea. She then said, "How about some Vicodin?" I told her she did not have enough Vicodin in the emergency room for me! She gave me an odd smile and went on talking about what she was seeing on my X-rays. I did fine taking Motrin and Tylenol and was truly amazed how well they relieved the pain. I learned a great deal that day. The biggest lesson was, I could deal with pain without narcotics. I remembered my withdrawal from opioids and the horror of my life before treatment. I had no desire to go back there. I also learned it would be very easy to go back down that road again, aided and abetted by a physician who was clueless about my disease.

Unfortunately, our medical schools provide little information about chemical dependency. To my knowledge, the schools provide absolutely no training on how to prescribe medication to the person in recovery. We spend hours and hours being taught about the medications that can be used and should be avoided in treating diabetes, heart disease, and so on. Until that changes, I will advise patients of their

139

responsibility to ask many questions before taking a prescription medication. People in recovery should not blame a doctor for relapses because it is up to them to accept responsibility for what they put into their body. Most treatment facilities provide a handout called "Cross Addiction," which provides a good set of guidelines for patients to follow. Over the years, I have seen hundreds of alcoholics who were sober for a period of time but later became addicted to Xanax, Vicodin, or Ambien. Many said they had no idea these medications could be a problem because they were just alcoholics. Remember, the nucleus accumbens does not really care what the drug is. Other patients had some inkling those prescriptions could pose a problem (they knew it intellectually), but they nonetheless believed that willpower and intelligence would get them through using the drug unscathed. Of course, they were wrong.

By the same token, it should not be a surprise that hundreds of "former drug addicts" have come to my office because of a "new" problem, namely, alcoholism. After battling drug addiction, the vast majority of patients who lose their sobriety relapse first on alcohol. Many return to their drug of choice over time, but some do not. Alcohol has replaced it.

The clearest example of this occurs with people addicted to cocaine. I tell all the cocaine addicts I see as patients that alcohol is potentially the most dangerous drug for them. I first get some odd looks, until I remind them of the times they had stopped using cocaine and then had a drink. I remind them that after a drink or two (or three), a little voice in their head will say, "It is OK to get just a little cocaine, only a gram. You can do a couple of lines and save the rest." It seems very logical, and then the plan unfolds. Alcohol kills inhibition; the rest is history.

The point is, chemically dependent individuals can relapse when they have no intention of doing so. I do not think anyone would argue that the medical profession very freely prescribes massive quantities of addictive drugs. Many of the state medical boards have begun to reprimand or punish physicians who overprescribe. Most of you realize there are "pill mills" disguised as medical clinics where addicts get easy access to prescription drugs. In almost every town, the addicts know which doctors ask the fewest questions and write the most prescriptions. These physicians are simply drug dealers. Some may eventually lose their medical licenses, but most will just move on to another town if they get into trouble. The vast majority of physicians do not fit this profile, though. They are caring, even the ones who are lax about overseeing and prescribing mood-altering drugs. Why? We were taught in medical school that there is a pill, powder, or liquid for anything that ails our patients. Many of us got too busy and found it easier to write prescriptions than sit and talk with patients. Every physician has given in to problem patients who complain constantly. Many of these patients are addicts and manipulators. They just bug the hell out of doctors until they get what they want. Some physicians just cannot say no to a patient. Addicts know this; they are truly masters at getting what they want.

Another huge problem has developed around penalties and punishment for over-prescribing. Inadequate treatment of pain has become a major issue for everyone, not only for chemically dependent patients in recovery. It is very important to remember that alcoholics and addicts in recovery have the right to pain treatment no different than the treatment afforded to other human beings. My patients often bring this up, and I assure them that they do not have to suffer because of their sobriety. If they have a surgical or medical procedure, they should receive the same quality of pain relief as anyone else. If Demerol is required to relieve their pain, they should have it. I first ran into a problem several years ago that sort of blew these assurances.

One of my patients called the office and told our nurse a story I cannot forget. The patient went into the hospital for abdominal pain, and she ended up needing an appendectomy. She told us that when she told her doctor she was in recovery for addiction, he refused to give her any pain medication. I did not review any hospital records, so I cannot verify this, but the patient had been sober for several years and was very reliable. I believe her story because I have heard many similar stories from other patients. A lack of education about chemical dependency has caused some doctors to compromise patients' medical care because of fear of prescribing medication to a "known addict." Why? Well, all physicians, I think, are aware they can lose their medical license for prescribing controlled substances to a known addict; the fear is real. I am not a lawyer, so I will avoid the politics in this issue. However, I suspect the law was meant to inhibit doctors from providing more drugs to drug addicts.

So what is the solution? At the end of my lectures, I advise patients that they have certain responsibilities. I tell them that, for simplicity sake, medical problems can be divided into two groups: Emergency and non-emergency situations.

1) Emergencies: Car wrecks, gunshot wounds, and major trauma.
If you are able to do so, let the medical staff know that you are in recovery. In some cases, the family may need to advise the staff. Do not worry about what medication(s) you are being given. If you are in pain and Demerol is the only drug available, take it, even if you were a Demerol addict. Ask your attending physician to request a consultation with someone in addiction medicine to help with your case, unless your attending doctor has been educated about addiction. The addiction medicine physician is only a consultant to your primary doctor. Interestingly, if you came to an emergency room with multiple traumas and informed the staff that you had diabetes or heart disease, a cardiologist, endocrinologist, or an internist would be consulted automatically. It is likely that if your primary doctor is an orthopedic surgeon, he or she requests a consultation because of a lack of expertise with these other diseases. It is unlikely that the primary physician will request a consultation with an addiction specialist if you simply tell them you are in recovery. That is why you have to ask for it.

Family members need to understand this because the patient may not be capable of making the request. In most cases, the consultation amounts to my telling the primary physician to give you the same medications the average person in your condition would receive. I also tell the physician to try not to prescribe opioids for my patients after they leave the hospital. This was possible years ago, but with our managed care system, you will be out on the street in a day or two. If further pain medications are needed, then a three- to five-day supply may be prescribed, with a family member or sober friend in charge of dispensing the medication. It is a really bad idea for you to dispense your own medication. I advise the primary doctor to prescribe medication for the average duration of time as for other patients.

The patient should have an appointment set up with the addictionologist before leaving the hospital. I have written a handout that is included in the appendices for patients who undergo surgery. After interviewing many patients who have had trauma or major surgical procedures, the vast majority will tell you that the pain medicine did not result in a high. It was taken for a different reason, and for most of them, the craving was not a major issue.

Here is the point to remember: It is not taking a mood-altering drug that causes a problem, it is how you go about doing it. You have not relapsed, and I encourage you to talk about the experience. It may help you someday — or others. Go to an AA or NA meeting right away. Talk openly about your experience so it does not become a secret.

2) Non-emergency medical problems.
Surprisingly, more people relapse from having a minor medical problem that may require pain medication or some type of sedation. Each year I see a large number of people who relapse from dental procedures. Dentists seem to have little or no training in chemical dependency. And fear of the dentist is high among patients.

Almost everyone I know seems to absolutely hate going to the dentist and would prefer "to be knocked out" if they have to go.

A few stitches, while painful, usually do not require sixty Vicodin with a refill, but this is not unheard of either. So how do you handle these problems? Here is a summary of my recommendations:

a) Let your medical professional know that you are in recovery.

b) Ask for a consultation with an addictionologist before the medical procedure, if possible.

c) Take the medications that are recommended by the professional.

d) After the consultation, your doctor will be advised to write prescriptions for small quantities of the medicine and to have someone else dispense it to you.

e) Seeing an addictionologist or your therapist, if you have one, is a good idea but not necessary.

f) You should go to an AA or NA meeting as promptly as you can and talk about the experience. Tell your sponsor about it. Just don't keep it a secret. It will help those who are at the meeting to know what to do if they face this issue. You just got a chance to do some service work, too.

Again, taking the medication is not a relapse, if properly handled. Do not let anyone convince you that you have failed!

In closing this chapter, I want to be clear to families and persons in recovery that going through a medical problem is very doable. Until we have adequate training for our medical professionals, you have to take on certain responsibilities and perhaps teach these professionals along the way. The vast majority of medical professionals are happy to learn from their patients. In many ways, those of us in recovery are pioneers in this disease of addiction. There is so much more to learn!

The lack of education about alcohol and drug addiction among attorneys, police officers, and judges is equivalent to that of the medical profession.

Chapter 17: The Criminal Justice System and the Disease

Most of the people incarcerated in our jails and prisons are there because of crimes involving the use of chemical substances. They often are arrested and charged with being under the influence, or they are caught stealing or robbing so they can support their addiction. Some people are caught selling drugs and report that they had to do it to maintain their own drug addiction. It is estimated that 80 percent to 85 percent of our prison population has the disease of chemical dependency. The lack of education about alcohol and drug addiction among attorneys, police officers, and judges is equivalent to that of the medical profession. Decisions by these professionals have a profound effect on the lives of many people — even after they leave prison. Most people do not realize that someone with a criminal record will have a very difficult time obtaining a job, renting a home, or being eligible to enter many professions. Having the disease of chemical dependency is not an excuse for criminal behavior.

In Texas, attempts to provide treatment for chemical dependency in our jail and prison system have been made by past governors. Laws were approved, but the funding was not. Some programs have been developed by the criminal justice system in the past few years. Leaders in the legal system believe these facilities and programs provide adequate treatment. I am sure they believe that in good faith, but without adequate knowledge of the disease, I am concerned that this is equivalent to the example I gave earlier. Would you prefer treatment for your cancer at the M.D. Anderson Cancer Center or would you choose a facility that provides unknown and unapproved herbs and chemicals? I have interviewed hundreds of patients who have been involved in the criminal justice model of treatment and most describe a punitive system that is vastly different from the therapeutic approach provided by private- and corporate-funded facilities. Most people would not choose to have a judge or attorney make medical decisions for them, nor would they choose a doctor to make legal decisions.

We all know that recidivism in the criminal justice system is very high. In my experience, I see untreated alcohol and drug addiction as being the greatest factor causing repeat criminal behavior and re-incarceration. It is time to take a careful look at this problem. Estimates show that the average cost of keeping someone in prison is $31,000 per year. Greed has infested so many areas of this "business" that it seems few people want to change a system that has remained the same for at least a hundred years. I am absolutely sure that good treatment could be provided so our society could be assured of a better form of crime prevention.

I also challenge the criminal justice system to consider the lifelong label of "convicted felon" and how that contributes to those who have this disease returning to the chemical they once used. Hundreds of people have criminal records and have long-term sobriety. The disturbing situation is, the man or woman who is incarcerated and has no opportunity to understand and pursue sobriety. They are released and face the frustration of having lost many of their rights, making it difficult to start over. It is no wonder that most return to crime.

Many others will not put forth the effort to live clean and sober, even with good treatment. Exposure to the truth about the disease really screws up their using. People who know the truth can never go back to their old life. They may not choose to pursue sobriety at that time, but at least the seed has been planted. Those who succeed will not likely return to the criminal justice system.

I believe society must look at these problems. I encourage our attorneys and judges to truly consider a rehabilitative approach for those struggling with addictions. This, of course, would require addicts to show proof that they are truly committed to changing their lives. They must earn back trust to regain the rights of every other human being. Most professionals in addiction medicine agree that the relapse rate is low for those who have been sober for five or more years. Sobriety is far bigger than abstinence. Ignorance is again the common denominator, so I challenge members of the legal profession to provide education for their colleagues. It will be difficult to change old ideas, but we must begin with the students who are still teachable.

I see a great deal of denial in the legal profession about members who may be impaired because of their alcohol or drug addiction. In Texas, there is no entity other than the State Bar that has the power to require treatment for an attorney. In the medical profession, peer assistance committees use leverage to get the impaired doctor, dentist, or nurse to enter treatment. These committees have no power to force the professional to seek treatment, but if the person refuses, the matter will go to the professional board for potential punishment. This is not the case with legal professionals in Texas. Its peer assistance program cannot turn the matter over to the Bar because of a confidentiality factor. That means some attorneys known to have this disease are allowed to continue making decisions that affect the lives of many people.

I am bringing up this issue to point out that all professions have enabled their alcohol- and drug-addicted members to practice, jeopardizing the health, safety and freedom of many others. The fact that the professional has this disease does not mean that he or she is impaired and unfit to work. The productivity decreases first and then poor decision-making and other problems follow.

I hope that through education all of our professionals can not only better help our patients or clients but also take better care of our own impaired colleagues in the process. Ignorance keeps those with addictions in fear; judgment and the secret can destroy them.

I have had the honor of being asked to intervene with a large number of medical doctors over the past two decades. The vast majority were thankful to see that they could stop the battle. The relief in their eyes was obvious. They, like me, did not understand that they were sick and had a treatable disease. They just thought they were bad or weak. As they recover, they will help others, and in the process, secure their own recovery. This is true for everyone, regardless of what they do for a living.

Suboxone is the harm reduction medication not the cure for opiod dependency.

Chapter 18: The Suboxone Breakthrough

In 2002, the U.S. Food and Drug Administration approved a medication named Suboxone, a breakthrough in addiction therapy. It is used by trained physicians to treat opioid-dependent people on an outpatient basis. Before this, only methadone was used. That usually amounted to a lateral move from illegal drugs, such as heroin or prescription painkillers, to a longer-acting opioid. It was moving from one drug to another in an effort to curb criminal activity, overdoses, HIV, hepatitis B infections, IV drug use, and other problems associated with opioid addiction. This method is often referred to as harm reduction.

Methadone can only be used under strict federal control and has helped many people.

Suboxone was approved for opioid detoxification and maintenance. I explain to patients on the first visit that Suboxone is to be used as a vehicle to help them into recovery. This was the intent of the pharmaceutical company that made the drug and of the federal government. But Suboxone is a complicated medication, and each physician certified to prescribe it must pass an examination after eight hours of training. Suboxone is odd: It is described as an

agonist and antagonist, which means it has one effect at a certain dose and an opposite effect at a different dosage. It is a remarkable medicine in many ways, but it also has its unique problems.

As I discussed in an earlier chapter, opioid withdrawal is extremely painful, and before Suboxone came along, we could only treat the withdrawal symptoms. Nothing seemed to help much. Suboxone changed that. It is a fascinating medication, but it, too, is an opioid, with a half-life of thirty-six hours. When prescribed correctly, Suboxone achieves three things in a very short time. The patient usually, within two hours, will experience no withdrawal symptoms and no craving for opioids. The person is functioning normally and is not intoxicated. The individual can work or attend school. It is almost magical! But all of the symptoms motivating the patient to seek help for the opioid addiction are eliminated. I have spent hours explaining to patients that the long-term goal is to get involved in a 12-step program. They need a support system to become chemically free from all mood-altering drugs, including Suboxone. I remind them, Suboxone is an opioid, and they are still dependent on opioids. They do not have to chase the high or avoid the withdrawal symptoms from short-acting opioids. They no longer have to worry about finding their drug dealer or live in constant fear of going into withdrawal. Things are better, but the problem is still there.

As I have mentioned, sobriety involves abstinence from mood-altering drugs. That requires changing behavior, thinking, and even beliefs. It is about working the 12 Steps and eventually helping others to become clean and sober. All of this takes effort. In the vast majority of cases, patients tell me during the second visit they cannot understand why it would be necessary to attend meetings because they feel so much better. The incentive to change has been wiped out.

In my initial office visit with patients, I point out that withdrawal from Suboxone is longer than the withdrawal from short-acting drugs, such as hydrocodone and heroin. The pharmaceutical company said the intensity of the withdrawal is not as onerous, and that may be true to some degree. But withdrawal from Suboxone will last two to three weeks, rather than seven to ten days, and the patients still feel miserable. The anxiety, depression, insomnia, and muscle aches are very difficult, but for patients who are active in 12-step meetings and have a support system, the withdrawal symptoms are tolerable. They can be successful in ending the opioid cycle. I am happy to say that I have seen a few patients achieve this goal. I am sorry to say that most have not been successful. I have tried many different approaches with dosing patients. The common problem is, most of these patients have not developed a substitute, such as recovery, to replace the drug. Some of this goes back to what I said earlier: Society considers it easier to take a pill than to change our lives. Patients simply don't understand the power of chemical dependency.

Most physicians who are certified to prescribe Suboxone have made valiant efforts to use the medication to assist their patients into sobriety. Most have faced the same problems I have seen. It is an ongoing battle to get patients to stop taking Suboxone. For a small percentage of patients who have used opioids for a long time, it is unlikely they will be able to function free of all chemicals. We believe that in these patients, the brain is incapable of producing enough of a substance called endorphins. The endorphins are the chemical normally produced in our brains that give us a sense of well-being. Opioids are similar in molecular structure to endorphins, so the brain's biofeedback mechanism used in producing endorphins comes to a halt. The body interprets injected or ingested opioids as endorphins. The feel-good factory shuts down, and if it is down for too long, it can't start back up. No timeline can show how long is too much, but after seven years of use, it is likely to be a problem. Maintenance therapy may be indicated when long-term use has interfered with the brain's ability to produce endorphins. Roughly, 3 percent to 5 percent of opioid addicts may require maintenance therapy. In these cases, Suboxone is replacing a substance that cannot be produced by the body because of prolonged opioid use. These patients are encouraged to develop a support group in AA or NA because they have to make changes. Again, if nothing changes, nothing changes.

I must admit it is sometimes difficult to determine who is a candidate for maintenance. This is a clinical decision that can be quite complicated. I believe patients and family members must be made to understand that Suboxone is not a magical solution. I suggest that any young person who has been dependent on opioid medication for less than a year not pursue it. Taking Suboxone is just postponing the inevitable.

A word of caution: A few doctors are in it for the money and will prescribe this medication as long as you keep paying for the office visits. There are bad apples in every barrel, but the majority of certified physicians have your best interest in mind. If you really want to achieve sobriety, ask questions about how long you might be on the medication. If there is no potential end point, find yourself another doctor.

In summary, if Suboxone is prescribed to you or a loved one for opioid addiction, things will improve, but only temporarily. There is no painless way to get through opioid withdrawal, period. Perhaps one will emerge someday, but I don't see that happening. I suggest you consider a good treatment program instead of trying to stop using opioids on your own. Most treatment centers use Suboxone to help with the initial detoxification, and when the Suboxone withdrawal begins, you will be in an environment to help you transition to sobriety.

In all honesty, getting off of opioids was the hardest thing I have ever done. Medical school was easy compared to this. If you think Suboxone is the answer to your problem, you are wrong. It is the best tool to come along thus far, but the core problem is still accepting the disease and being willing to change behaviors and attitudes. If there is a medication discovered to remedy this disease, I will be out of a job. And that would be great!

Do not base your choice on cost.

Chapter 19: How to Find a Treatment Center

Choosing a treatment program is a big topic, so I will focus on the key issues to consider.

Be really careful about deciding on your own what type of treatment is best for you or your loved one. Doing this would be much like picking what you think would be the most effective chemotherapy for your cancer. The best suggestion I can offer is to meet with an addictionologist or a knowledgeable therapist for recommendations. As I said earlier, everyone is different, and every treatment center is different, although the basic philosophy may be the same. Just because a treatment facility has been around for a number of years and you have heard the name a few times does not make it the best choice. Going through the yellow pages is not a good idea. Most treatment centers were set up to be thirty-day programs because the first ones were mainly for treating alcoholics. The withdrawal period from alcohol is about thirty days. If you are using a substance with a long half-life like an opioid, a thirty-day program may not be the best choice.

Keeping these points in mind, here are some suggestions:

1) A well-known facility may be good because it has been around for a long time, but don't assume it's best for you or your loved one.

2) Get guidance from someone who has worked in the addiction field. Most experienced professionals can at least caution you about inappropriate centers.

If you know of someone who has been to a particular treatment facility, call him or her. Of course, calling someone who is still sober would be the best idea!

3) Do not base your choice on cost. Expensive facilities are usually no better than lower-cost ones. The expensive facilities offer more fluff, which I guess might work for some people. No facility has come up with a secret formula for sobriety, so the old phase of getting what you pay for does not work here. Costs range widely among centers of equal caliber.

4) Look at the websites for the facilities but understand that anyone can make something sound or look good.

5) Call the facility you are interested in and ask for the intake coordinator. Don't be shy about asking questions or calling back as more arise. It may take two or three calls to answer your questions. All good facilities have a waiting list and have no interest in selling you anything. They can also answer insurance coverage questions.

Ask about payment plans and scholarships because some good programs will work with you financially. They believe that if they do a good job and you stay sober, you will pay them back. Good philosophy!

6) Do not worry about the facility's location. Speaking from my experience, I think the farther you are from home, the less crap you have to deal with. You are getting help for a fatal disease so you do not need much outside distraction. Most patients want to stay close to home, but for what? In my opinion, the farther you are from your family and job, the better your prognosis.

7) Be sure to ask if there is a formal family program; all reputable facilities have one. The family has a right to get help, too, and it will make your life much easier if they can begin to understand the disease better. Entering treatment is seldom really an emergency, so ask a lot of questions so you can have confidence in your decision. Because an addict tells you one day he or she is willing to go to treatment doesn't mean the person has reached bottom. It could be a maneuver to get you to back off, and the person's attitude may be different tomorrow. Someone who is

beaten by this disease still will be ready the next day or week. The sooner, the better, of course, but timing is a very important decision for everyone involved.

8) No treatment center is perfect. A positive outcome will only occur if the patient is willing to follow through with the recommendations. Facilities don't work; it is the patient who chooses whether to work.

9) Whatever facility you choose, your loved one will call you in about two days to tell you how the choice was a big mistake. Being new in treatment is terrifying, and even the most committed patients will magnify any flaw or inconsistency they can possibly find. The stories are fascinating to hear and you, the family member, will be tempted to jump in your car and go to the rescue. Encourage your loved one to be patient and open-minded. Be supportive, but don't bail them out. That has never worked. The members of the treatment team will do their work, so let them!

10) Lastly, do not decide on inpatient or outpatient treatment without obtaining information first. Outpatient treatment works very well for some people. All respectable outpatient programs do an assessment before accepting anyone to make sure that type of treatment is appropriate for the patient. Inpatient programs also do assessments, and, in some cases, may recommend outpatient treatment instead. Such safeguards are designed to appropriately match the patient to the center.

Inpatient versus Outpatient

Almost every patient will choose outpatient instead of inpatient treatment because it causes the least amount of disruption. The fear of losing a job is usually the biggest reason. Many consider it an easier way to "deal with the problem." Family members often support this choice because it is less expensive — and less inconvenient. Often, they think they can keep the secret and avoid the embarrassment if their loved one is treated as an outpatient. The choice works for many people, and while the examples I cited aren't the best reasons, I have learned not to predict who will be successful and who will fail as an outpatient. The most critical step is changing the person's behavior.

The intake assessment will decide which setting is best, but here are general guidelines for trying to decide if someone is a good candidate for outpatient treatment. Such individuals are:

a) Motivated to change.

b) Employed. This is not mandatory, but idle time is an addict's enemy.

c) Able to count on support, either from family or others who care about them.

d) Not at risk for medical problems during detoxification.

e) Free of a mental illness, which could prevent them from understanding and processing information.

f) Equipped with the necessary transportation and a schedule that allows them to be on time and present for every session.

h) Medically stable.

i) Not taking mood-altering drugs, such as pain pills, while recovering from a recent surgery.

Please note that in item (d) I mentioned medical risk with detoxification. I have discussed previously that some drugs, because of their fat solubility, will cause a prolonged withdrawal. That must be considered when choosing between inpatient or outpatient treatment. I see many patients on benzodiazepines and opioids who attempt a week of inpatient care before moving to an outpatient program. Have you ever hit your thumb with a hammer and had a nanosecond or two before the pain hit? Sounds odd, but that is a good example of the need to allow enough time

159

in the proper setting. Some people are successful at transitioning quickly, but it takes great effort and determination.

I am truly surprised and almost speechless when someone accepts the recommendation for inpatient treatment. Centers provide thirty-, sixty-, and ninety-day programs. Some are even longer. Generally speaking, all of them phase the patient from inpatient to outpatient and then to residential living. They really are not what most people think of as being institutionalized for a long time.

On the other hand, inpatient programs are best for patients who:

a) Have been unable to stay sober after outpatient treatment.

b) Have risks for medical problems from their withdrawal.

c) Have a coexisting psychiatric disorder that is under reasonable control.

d) Have been unable to stop using despite repeated, serious attempts.

e) Need a safe environment from a living situation that is dangerous to sobriety (i.e., a cocaine addict who lives next door to a crack house or an alcoholic who lives in a family with active alcoholics).

Motivation is always important but less so during inpatient treatment. Attitude can change dramatically in a short time.

These lists are not at all complete because each person can have a combination of problems or unique circumstances that must be considered. That is why I said matching a person to the right treatment is very important. I can offer my opinion, but I have never been able to guarantee a patient or family my recommendations will work. The patient's motivation is the key factor. Finally, and this is only my opinion, I think it is much easier to get sober in a long-term residential program than in an outpatient program. The only thing people in treatment have to focus on is themselves and their recovery. This is very unpleasant at first because everyone

160

else is focusing on them, too. They have a lot of time to think about what is being said and will be very busy from 6:00 a.m. to 9:00 p.m., if they are truly participating. They will have little to no time to hang out with their worst enemy — themselves. They are free of job stresses because they are not working at the moment. They also are free of dealing with the ongoing insanity of their family. They do not have to worry about their drug dealer stopping by or calling or a friend dropping by with "the best weed or cocaine ever." They do not have to worry about meals because that is part of the package. They are with a group of people who they do not have to impress because everyone has the same disease. Some of the people have been there longer and are on fire! They are happy and hopeful. The newcomer begins to think, "If they can do this, so can I." No one in this group is there to shame anyone, and no matter how bad some people might think they are, someone else has a better story. People in residential care learn how to communicate with others using words that are longer than four letters. They have come to understand that having feelings is OK and won't kill them. Eventually, they come to understand that they were sick and that they were not a bad person. That's a gift no one can take away.

I have learned that I can only do so much to alter the course of someone else's life.

CHAPTER 20: Closing Thoughts

I have done my best to share with you what I have learned from some very remarkable people.

I have had the best job anyone could want. I have had the honor of being someone who, for whatever reason, people have trusted. They tell me about their lives, good and bad. I have witnessed some of the most incredible miracles anyone could imagine. I have seen so many die, including the young. I could not comprehend the pain a parent experiences when their son or daughter dies from this damn disease.

I have learned that I can only do so much to alter the course of someone else's life. I can plant the seed of sobriety, but I cannot make it grow. I cannot describe the joy that I experience when a patient I have not seen in years walks into my office to introduce their family and tells me of the happiness they have found. Nor can I describe the pain when a parent or spouse calls to tell me their loved one has died from an overdose or a car wreck caused by drugging or drinking.

I have never been bored doing this work. Just when I think I have heard it all, someone reminds me I have not. There are many days when I hate this disease because it is more powerful than love, honor, and integrity. I have had to accept that I cannot make a patient want this wonderful gift called sobriety. I do not know why some make it and others don't. We understand so much more today about this disease, but the truth is, we still don't know enough. I often wonder how many people have spent their lives in hell, never knowing a solution exists. They died believing they were bad, stupid, or defective in some way. How many families spend years wondering whether they caused their loved one to despair or why they couldn't have done something to save them?

Almost every member of the family I was raised in died from this disease. I'm sure they never knew there was another way. I hope and pray that the information in this book will help someone break the cycle of turning away and ignoring the problem. I hope our medical profession someday realizes how much more they could do to help so many people. Think of the number of lives that would be affected if our medical students really understood this disease and how to treat it. It must start with the students before they come to believe that alcoholics and addicts are just defective people. Family members can quit enabling their loved ones and be a part of killing this secret.

It seems that very few people have an interest in addiction unless someone they love dearly has this disease and that person's behavior directly affects them. Having an acquaintance or a friend of the family who has a drug problem does not usually elicit enough emotional discomfort to cause someone to seek information about addiction. This is human nature and likely is the same attitude people adopt when they hear about other medical diseases. The difference, though, is that many people have more deeply ingrained prejudices about alcohol and drug addiction.

As I write this, I just finished meeting with a physician who had completed addiction treatment and was preparing to transition back to his home and job. When he met with his partners yesterday to discuss his return to work, one of them told him that he hoped that he was remorseful for what he had done. I am thankful I had the opportunity to remind this physician that his partner's statement, while hurtful, was due to ignorance. I told him he would face other situations like this in the future. I also reminded him that, what had seemed to be such a liability (his disease), would be one of his greatest assets as a physician. I believe he will be one more person who will have the opportunity to help change the old beliefs.

The old beliefs have maintained secrecy, shame, and despair. They have overshadowed the fact that there is a solution to alcohol and drug addiction. It is a treatable disease for anyone who has the desire and who asks for help. I hope this book will help open the door to the closet so that someday, everyone who has this disease has the opportunity to be free and at peace. If you are reading this book and you are someone who has this disease, I am going to make you a promise. If you are willing to be honest, willing to put forth effort, and willing to look deep inside of yourself and find that little glimmer of hope, you will attain happiness, peace, and freedom far greater than you could imagine. No one can take that from you. Ever. May God bless you on this journey.

Afterword

Dr. Herbert C. "Butch" Munden died of prostate cancer Oct. 24, 2016, at age 66. The loss was deeply felt in the community he had served for so many years. But it was comforting to know Butch would have enjoyed his memorial service. So many people he had helped as a pioneering addiction specialist in Austin for thirty years packed the 232-seat auditorium at the Lady Bird Johnson Wildflower Center. It was standing room only. For a couple of hours that afternoon, one person after next stood at the lectern to talk about Butch, some with voices cracking. He had seen them at their worst, but he never judged.

"Butch saved my life," said one of the many doctors who spoke openly that day about his journey with addiction. Others who followed him at the lectern included Butch's friends and blue-collar workers. All unabashedly expressed their love for the man who helped them get sober. He brought them back from the brink of despair and never stopped believing in them, they said.

Butch understood them like few others could because, for eighteen years, he had walked the same path. He sought addiction treatment four days after he missed his daughter's fifth birthday party to buy drugs. He was a physician but didn't realize until then how far his life had spun out of control. He feared he would lose his family. So he got well. At the memorial service, Butch would have been pleased to hear his three adult children tell stories about his quirks, love of adventure, and the fun he brought to their lives. They were proud to call Butch their father.

I was privileged to have known Butch and honored when his wife, Hannah, called me after the November 10 service to update and edit this book.

Butch had told me his own inspiring story of addiction and recovery a dozen or so years earlier. He spoke openly and honestly about it. Helping other addicts reclaim their lives had become his passion. Not long after he completed treatment in 1985, he traded his family medicine practice for a specialty in addiction therapy. He abhorred the shame and secrecy that makes addiction so hard to address. His story appeared on the front page of the Austin American-Statesman. He hoped it would nudge other addicts into treatment.

From that point on, Butch was my "go-to" person when I wrote about chemical dependency. He was always generous with his time, patiently explaining the complexities and nuances surrounding addiction. For him, it was about giving back. He wanted to help individuals and families suffering from alcoholism and drug addiction. He was dedicated to showing them that there was another way, that a happier, more peaceful life was within their reach. Because he cared, he left a lasting imprint on his community — and beyond. We are better because of him.

— Mary Ann Roser, Austin, Texas   June 30, 2017

Acknowledgements

Thanks to the thousands of patients and family members who taught me so much. So many people converted my inspiration into a readable book. I am from East Texas, and many people say my mind works differently than the English language. My deepest thanks to my wife, Hannah, for the endless hours she put into this endeavor. She is the only person who was able to convince me that my stream-of-consciousness writing style did not make sense to most people. All of this material was handwritten, and I am grateful to Julia Kirchen Sweeney for the patience it took to decipher my chicken scratch. I truly appreciate the efforts of Gena VanOsselear who spent endless hours editing this manuscript. Gena has known me long enough to put my thinking into words that make sense. All three of my children — Vanessa, Shannon, and Marshall — made contributions, and I appreciate their patience with me during these months. Donna Dornak helped so much by listening to me and giving me endless encouragement when I doubted myself. Many others, too numerous to call out, cheered me on and believed in me. And lastly, but certainly not least, I thank my sponsor, Charles, for having the patience of Job. Thanks also to Jim Weigel whose rudeness and sarcasm made me want to stay sober just to prove him wrong. You are the best, Jim!

Glossary

Abuse – The overuse of alcohol and/or drugs. Individuals voluntarily and purposefully overuse. This use may cause consequences; however, the individual can and often will stop or diminish use in response to the consequences.

Addiction – A condition that occurs when a person continues to use alcohol and/or drugs despite it causing negative consequences in their lives. They simply can't stop using.

Alcoholics Anonymous – A worldwide fellowship of men and women who have meetings for the purpose of getting sober, maintaining it and helping others achieve sobriety. The program was founded in 1935 and there are 12 Steps used by members to achieve sobriety. Anonymity of members is the spiritual foundation of the program.

Amygdala – An area of the brain that is part of the dopamine (reward or pleasure) system where chemical dependency originates. It is responsible for the storage of positive and negative emotional memory.

Benzodiazepines – A class of drugs used to treat anxiety and multiple other medical conditions. Valium is the brand name for the first commercially produced benzodiazepine.

Craving – The urge or desire to use a drug or alcohol. This is a very subjective term. Craving does not mean dependency.

Cross-addiction – Occurs when someone is addicted to one drug that they stop using but become dependent on another drug because the effect on the brain is the same. This term will likely disappear because we now know that the malfunction in the mesolimbic brain which "doesn't care what drug it is." As long as the drug releases dopamine from the nucleus accumbens, the addiction will occur.

Dopamine – A chemical in the brain that is a neurotransmitter. This substance allows signals to be passed on to other nerves. This particular neurotransmitter is involved with pleasure and emotional responses.

EMDR – Acronym for eye movement desensitization and reprocessing. A form of psychotherapy used to resolve the development of trauma-related disorders caused by exposure to distressing or negative life events. It is used to adapt to dysfunctional thinking stored in the brain's memory center.

Endorphins – Substances that are naturally produced in the body with a chemical structure similar to morphine. They are involved with pain regulation and the sense of well -being.

Hallucination – An altered perception of reality that has no external cause but can involve the sense of smell, vision, and/or sound.

Mesolimbic dopamine system – The reward pathway of the brain. It consists of two functional areas: the nucleus accumbens and the ventral tegmental area.

Multifactorial – The involvement of different causes, circumstances or reasons that contribute to a problem, such as addiction.

Normal – Refers here to individuals who are not chemically dependent. It is also used to describe behavior that is common in people who do not have an addiction or another pathology.

Nucleus accumbens – A powerful part of the mesolimbic brain that is primarily involved in releasing dopamine.

Withdrawal syndrome – A constellation of symptoms that occur when the dose of an addictive drug is stopped or markedly decreased. The symptoms are the opposite of the initial effect of the drug, indicating that the body has adapted to the drug.

OPIOID FACT SHEET

What are opioids?

Generally known as painkillers, opioids include illegal drugs, such as heroin, as well as prescription pain medications, such as codeine, hydrocodone (Lortab, Norco, Vicodin), fentanyl (Duragesic, Fentora), morphine, hydromorphone (Dilaudid, Exalgo), methadone, and oxycodone (OxyContin, Percodan, Percocet).

In addition, buprenorphine (Subutex) is an opioid that is used to treat opioid addiction. It works as a treatment by limiting the euphoria opioid users crave, thus lowering the potential for abuse. It also suppresses symptoms of withdrawal. Another treatment is Suboxone, a combination of buprenorphine and naloxone, a prescription medicine used to block the effects of an opioid and reverse an opioid overdose.

Opioids can be manufactured with chemicals or derived naturally from the opium poppy. Whether synthetic or natural, opioids work by binding to specific receptors in the brain, spinal cord, and gastrointestinal tract. The process of binding to the body's pain receptors results in minimizing the body's perception of pain. Opioids also stimulate the "reward centers" in the brain, inducing a feeling of euphoria. However, opioids can be deadly given their sedating effect. They can lower blood pressure and slow or stop a person's breathing.

How do opioids affect people, society?

Affects vary after a person takes opioids, ranging from pleasure to nausea, vomiting, slowed heartbeat, and reduced breathing. When the body becomes overwhelmed by the opioid, an overdose can occur.

While addicts face the highest risk of overdosing, an overdose can happen to anyone who takes more than the prescribed amount of the drug or uses it with other drugs, including alcohol.

In recent years, opioid overdoses have reached epidemic proportions, especially among users of heroin and prescription medications, such as oxycodone, hydrocodone, morphine, and fentanyl. In 2016, the leading cause of death in people under fifty was an opioid overdose. That year, officials estimate that between fifty-nine thousand and sixty-five thousand Americans died of an overdose.

Leading reasons for the epidemic include an increase in pain medicine prescriptions, the availability of illegal drugs, and the ease of obtaining drugs over the Internet. Because of the prevalence of overdoses in America, laws are changing in various states to make it easier to rescue a loved one from an overdose.

For example, in Texas the Overdose Awareness Group provides free boxes of Ezvio, the injectable form of naloxone. These "auto-injectors" come with a practice injector and one with naloxone. Ezvio rapidly delivers a single dose of naloxone to reverse an overdose. It is legal in Texas to have these auto-injectors for emergency use.

If you don't know the laws in your state on obtaining naloxone, contact a drug overdose awareness organization in your state or do research using the Internet. You can also ask your family doctor for a prescription for naloxone, and the pharmacist should be able to help with details on administering it. Always check the expiration date on the box and make sure it has not expired.

How can you help someone who has overdosed?

Step 1. Every minute matters:

1. Call 911 immediately.
2. Give the dispatcher the address and report, "Someone is not breathing."

Step 2. Be aware of symptoms that may progress to an overdose, including:

1. Unusual sleepiness or drowsiness.
2. Mental confusion, slurred speech, or other intoxicated behavior.
3. Pupils that are pinpoint small.
4. Slowed heartbeat or lowered blood pressure.
5. Difficulty waking the person from sleep.

Step 3. Check for signs of an opioid overdose. They include:

1. The face is extremely pale or clammy.

2. The body is limp.

3. The person cannot be awakened from sleep or is unable to speak.
4. Breathing is very slow or has stopped.
5. The pulse, or heartbeat, is very slow or has stopped.
6. Hearing a "death rattle," an exhaled breath with a distinct, labored sound coming from the throat. This indicates that you should begin emergency resuscitation; it almost always means the person is near death.

Step 4. If there is no oxygen available and the person is having trouble breathing, you will need to provide emergency resuscitation.

1. Make sure the person's airway is clear. This means checking to see that nothing is in the mouth or throat blocking the airway.
2. Place one of your hands on the person's chin, tilt the head back, and pinch the nose closed.
3. Place your mouth over the person's mouth to make a seal and give two slow breaths.
4. The person's chest should rise but not the stomach.
5. Follow up with one breath every five seconds.

Step 5: Administer naloxone (Narcan), if available, to reverse the overdose:

1. Understand that naloxone is for opioid overdoses and is not effective in treating overdoses of benzodiazepines, sedatives, stimulants, GHB, or Ecstasy. It can be helpful in overdoses involving drugs taken in combination with opioids.
2. Because it takes three to five minutes for naloxone to work, continue assisted breathing until the person's normal breathing returns.
3. If the person becomes combative or feels uneasy as the medication becomes effective, help them remain calm. Monitor the person and make them as comfortable as possible until the ambulance arrives.
4. The emergency room doctor needs to be told what is suspected of causing the overdose and any other details you may have about the person's medical condition, including other medications he or she may be taking.

Post Operative Pain Management

What patients must understand

First and foremost, a person in addiction recovery does not need to suffer or be denied medication because of their chemical dependency. However, when addictive-type medications may be necessary, such as during or after surgery, the patient must take certain responsibilities to prevent a relapse.

The risk for relapse is high in these situations. Yet the vast majority of patients underestimate the risk, which is a major factor in the high relapse rate among addicts. Most erroneously believe that because they have been sober for a period of time, they will "know" how to handle the situation. Some who consider themselves "alcoholics" only, are at a very high risk because of cross-addiction. History has shown and research supports the fact that addiction is a brain disease called chemical dependency. Any addictive substance (those that stimulate the brain's reward center, or nucleus accumbens) has the potential to cause a relapse. To be clear, it is not the drug or chemical itself, it is the brain's reaction to the substance that matters.

The term "surgery" encompasses a wide variety of possibilities from open-heart surgery, joint replacement, appendectomy, to minor surgeries, such as a skin biopsy or dental procedure. But even a minor procedure can cause a major relapse. Most patients assume that their doctor or dentist "knows" about their addiction and how to handle it. They should not assume that. Further, the vast majority of medical professionals have had little, if any, training in chemical dependency. Even worse, most have had no training in how and what to prescribe to someone in recovery.

Patients must advise the medical professional that they have a disease that may be affected by prescribed medication. This is the patient's responsibility. The patient also should ask whether the medical professional has experience in prescribing to people with chemical dependencies. If the answer is no, the patient should suggest the medical professional consult with an addiction medicine specialist before the surgical procedure. This can be uncomfortable for the patient and the doctor. But failing to be assertive can have drastic consequences. Further, family members, sponsors, or trusted friends should be a part of this process. Secrecy is the first step on the road to relapse.

In sum:

> 1. Patients should not underestimate the high risk of relapse when taking certain medications.
> 2. Regardless of a person's drug of choice, patients must remember that the brain is the problem, not the chemical.
> 3. Most medical professionals have little or no training about the disease of chemical dependency. Until that changes, the patient is responsible for making sure they get proper medical care.
> 4. Patients need to have others involved at the beginning of the process. They should not face the issue alone.

Preparation

Before surgery, patients in recovery should talk about exposure to certain medications in AA meetings and with their sponsors. It is quite natural for some to "look forward" to using or getting high again. Patients need not waste time feeling guilty about this. Instead, they need to talk to others, including peers who have had similar experiences. Patients should understand that medications prescribed for true pain have a different effect than when they used drugs to get high. They

176

should look honestly at their expectations and not be fearful as long as they fully respect and understand the process.

Before surgery, patients should designate a trusted person who can dispense their medication after they leave the hospital or surgery center. If necessary, the designated person may need a lockbox for the medication so the patient does not have access to it. The dispensing person should be instructed to provide the medication strictly as it is written on the prescription. This person should not make any medical decisions. If problems arise, the doctor should be called. Communication with medical professionals is very important during the post-surgical period. There are no clear rules about who should dispense your medication. The patient's spouse or dearest loved one is usually not the best candidate because this is not an easy task. In the ideal situation, a trained professional (in-home health nurse) would visit daily and dispense a 24-hour supply of the medication, separated in individualized dosage containers. Patients must be honest with whoever is dispensing the medicine and should have their sponsor or other AA/NA members visit if they can't attend meetings. Once they are well enough, patients should get back to their meetings ASAP and talk about their experience. This may help others.

Patients should always ask about and use all other appropriate means of reducing pain rather than simply depending on medications. Acupuncture, electro stimulation, topical local anesthetics, and non-narcotic analgesics are examples. They should ask their physician about these options before the surgery. After surgery, if physical therapy has been recommended, they should do it.

Regardless of the reason, once a person's brain is exposed to these types of medications, the person's thinking will change to some degree, but he or she won't realize it. The addictive behaviors, rationalizations, projections, and blaming may resurface, in part because the brain is changed chemically. These behaviors are stepping-stones to relapse. That's why patients need to stay connected to their support groups and be willing to have someone point out concerns to them.

A medical professional may be available to consult with the patient's physician, as long as the patient and doctor agree. This medical consultation should begin well before surgery. In most cases, the consulting physician will not manage the acute phase of the post-operative pain, which can last from 24 hours to several weeks. There are no hard-and-fast rules for this phase of recovery, but a general guideline will be provided. Each person is different so the plan must be malleable.

In sum, patients should:

1. Plan ahead.
2. Be participants in the process.
3. Be open to alternatives besides medication.
4. Request a consultation.
5. Not underestimate the power of what they are facing.

The consultant's protocol

A consulting physician works with and does not replace the patient's doctor.

Post-operative pain management is not precise, but to be successful, it will involve discussions between the addiction medicine specialist and the primary (surgeon) doctor. Patients will need to ask the physician to sign and fill out a very short form included with this document. Patients should do this before surgery, preferably two weeks out.

Although the patient's physician or surgeon cannot know the outcome of the patient's surgery in advance, the patient will have a general idea of how medication will be prescribed. Patients must know this ahead of time so they can make goals rather than adopting an open-ended mindset.

Form for Doctors

(this form is to be given to your addictionologist or primary practitioner. They put their contact information at the top of the form and then fax it to the doctor or dentist who will be prescribing the pain medication post op.) example:

From:(Herbert C. Munden M.D

2100 Kramer Lane

Austin, TX) 78758

_____

Date: _____

To: (Name of surgeon)

_____M.D.

I appreciate the opportunity to consult with you regarding patient, (name)

_____ concerning his/her post-op pain management. Generally, the consultation (prescribing, etc.) will begin after the acute pain phase that will be determined by you. Each patient's situation will vary but please answer the questions below to help us determine general guidelines. Your experience is so important.

1. Acute post-op time period: _____ days, or _____ weeks

2. Please indicate date that you would suggest the consultation to begin:

_____ (day/month/year)

3. Please estimate the average duration that most patients with this type of surgery will require pain medication. Indicate, if possible, when you would normally begin a transition to non-opioid medication.

Average duration of opioid type medication_____ days, or _____ weeks.

Transition to non-opioid medication _____ days, or _____ weeks.

Sincerely,

Dr. _____

Enter either door and come out the Butterfly!

Made in the USA
Coppell, TX
24 September 2022

83548988R00101